THE KINGDOM
REVEALED

A DEVOTIONAL STUDY ON
THE SERMON ON THE MOUNT

D0107856

ALLEN SATTERLEE

wesleyan
PUBLISHING HOUSE
wphstore.com
Indianapolis, Indiana

CREST BOOKS

Copyright © 2018 by The Salvation Army National Corporation
Published by Wesleyan Publishing House
Indianapolis, Indiana 46250
Printed in the United States of America
ISBN: 978-1-63257-270-7
ISBN (e-book): 978-1-63257-271-4

All Scripture quotations, unless otherwise indicated, are taken from
the Holy Bible, New International Version®, NIV ®. Copyright
©1973, 1978, 1984, 2011 by Biblica, Inc. Used by permission of
Zondervan. All rights reserved worldwide. www.zondervan.com. The
"NIV" and "New International Version" are trademarks registered in
the United States Patent and Trademark Office by Biblica, Inc.

Scripture quotations marked (NLT) are taken from the Holy Bible,
New Living Translation, copyright © 1996, 2004, 2007, 2013 by
Tyndale House Foundation. Used by permission of Tyndale House
Publishers, Inc., Carol Stream, Illinois 60188. All rights reserved.

All rights reserved. No part of this publication may be reproduced,
stored in a retrieval system, or transmitted in any form or by any
means—electronic, mechanical, photocopy, recording, or any
other—except for brief quotations in printed reviews, without the
prior written permission of the publisher.

CONTENTS

INTRODUCTION

Over the centuries, the Sermon on the Mount (see Matt. 5–7) has been one of the most preached, taught, studied, and dissected passages of Scripture. You can find numerous views on it. Some feel that the sermon simply presents an ideal, but because its demands are so high, it is an ideal impossible to live. Others believe that the sermon describes life in God's kingdom following Christ's return. The early church, both in the Western and Eastern traditions, interpreted the Sermon on the Mount as a description of how to live the Christian life in the present.

In this study, we agree with the early church, viewing the Sermon on the Mount as a comprehensive description of how to live the Christian life — a life of holiness — today.

If the Sermon on the Mount did not have application in the present life, then Jesus set before us teachings that will only cause frustration. Just as the Jewish nation struggled to obey the law given through Moses, we would struggle even more to follow Christ's teachings, becoming trapped in a cycle of occasional obedience and frequent failure. In light of the gospel of grace and the assurance of God's loving care, the Sermon on the Mount would seem a cruel joke.

But that is not what it is. Just as the Law described what living up to God's standards looks like, the Sermon on the Mount shows us the character of the Christian life, the holy life. Oswald Chambers wrote, "The Sermon on the Mount is a statement of the life we will live when the Holy Spirit is having His way with us."[1]

When we read this Scripture passage and carefully consider what it says, we can feel quite overwhelmed. We find ourselves constantly doing a mental check: *Do I act this way? When have I treated others like this? When God looks in my heart, what does He see?* Any sincere Christian wants his life and heart in sync with the Lord so that he can properly be salt and light to the world.

But unlike the people in the Old Testament days, we are not left to our own strength and wisdom. "If you, then, though you are evil, know how to give good gifts to your children, how much more will your Father in heaven give good gifts to those who ask him!" (Matt. 7:11). God will not frustrate our holy desires but provide the means to achieve them. When the Holy Spirit is free to move within a heart that is fully yielded to Him, He gently reveals when we move away from humility, when we are tempted to retaliate. He helps us turn the other cheek and sets our ambitions on the things of God for His glory.

As you read this book, know that each verse applies to you in your present-day walk with the Lord. If you feel that you have fallen short, seek the Lord before you do anything else. God wants you to be whole and complete in Him. He stands ready to take you where you are, to lead you where you need to go.

1

LITTLE IS MUCH

MATTHEW 5:3

Captain Michael was the leader of a Salvation Army district that was growing rapidly in Papua New Guinea. One day a fellow officer said to him, "Captain B says that, as your second-in-command, he is your assistant."

Captain Michael replied, "Why would he want to be that? I am nothing, less than nothing. So, if he says he is my assistant, it means he is less than I am. How could that be?"

The captain's response fell in line with the deep, unconscious humility that seemed to characterize our Papua New Guinea officers. Jesus might have described this leader as "poor in spirit," meaning that he sought no glory for himself, realized his weakness, and knew that everything he accomplished was through the grace and strength of the Lord.

Perhaps being "poor in spirit" was key to that officer's growth. But doesn't this attitude seem to clash with today's standards? For example, in applying for a job, you are expected to present your résumé. You outline your work experience, education, skills, honors or awards, and present yourself as someone who is a strong candidate for the job. That is the way things work in this world. But the kingdom works with totally different criteria.

In Matthew 5:3, Jesus laid down a shocking, counter-cultural, counterintuitive guideline for what it means to be in the kingdom. Because being poor in spirit is so against our natural inclinations, it takes some wrestling to grasp what it means.

To be poor in spirit is to realize that you can do absolutely nothing that commands God's acceptance. All our clothes are tattered and filthy. All our works are smoke and ashes. We are more than bankrupt, because we carry a debt that all our wages for a thousand years can never reduce. If we presented our résumé to God, it would appear like a three-year-old's scribblings next to a Rembrandt. If we sang Him our songs, they would sound like horrid screeching compared to Mozart's symphonies.

We dare not plead our case because we are unquestion-ably guilty in God's sight and the sight of any who know us. It matters not where others stand before God because we cannot see beyond our own wretched unworthiness.

Like a man at the end of his strength who is being drawn out to sea by the currents, we cannot effect our own rescue. That is what we mean by total depravity and that is precisely where we are before the grace of God reaches us.

Strangely, sin is so self-deceiving that it is unnatural for us to see our condition on our own. We try to justify why we are deserving, why our happiness matters so much in the great scheme of things, why we should receive the award or the recognition. We quickly turn away from moments of self-reckoning and tell ourselves that we're doing just fine.

The Holy Spirit not only reveals to us who God is but also shows us who we are and why we so desperately need Him. And as miserable as that moment of revelation might be, it is of utmost importance. Entrance to the kingdom comes through this door and no other.

Being poor in spirit is surprisingly liberating. As the great writer and missionary, E. Stanley Jones said, "In the bath of renunciation he (the penitent) has washed his soul clean from a thousand clamoring, conflicting desires. Asking for nothing, if anything comes to him, it is all sheer gain."[1]

When considering what it means to be poor in spirit, it is important to realize that Jesus was not referring to material poverty. There are people who are desperately poor, but who know nothing of humility. And there are very wealthy people who are fully aware of their utter need of grace and are truly humble. Poverty in itself is not virtuous. If it were, we would be wrong to help the poor because in doing so we would rob them of their blessing.

Despite this, a person who is materially poor is more likely to be aware of his own limitations and of what he lacks more quickly than someone who is well off. Jesus summed up this fact up neatly when He said, "It is easier for a camel to go through the eye of a needle than for someone who is rich to enter the kingdom of God" (Matt. 19:24).

Poorness in spirit is not only needed to enter the kingdom of God but must be a continuing attitude in the Christian walk. Nothing is more insufferable than a self-righteous believer. As we grow in maturity and holiness, we find not that we are more self-assured, but that we become more aware of the awfulness of sin and of how vulnerable we are to the dangers in the world. We should grow as abhorrent of sin in our own lives as of sin in the unredeemed world. Salvation does not place us in a position of "holier than thou" judgment, but of genuine grief that anyone lives without Christ, either knowingly offending Him or living without regard to Him. We remain poor in spirit not only because of what we were, but also because of what we'd be capable of, were it not for Christ. We know that we could be in the place of the vilest criminal were it not for God's grace.

The poor in spirit are blessed, "for theirs is the kingdom of God." What does that mean?

We have only glimpses of what eternity will look like. Just as Peter cried out when he realized he could not save himself, we cry out, "Lord, save me!" (Matt. 14:30). We seek to walk obediently before Him, ever on guard against anything that might distract us from full allegiance to our Lord. Like Paul we aim "that in everything He might have the supremacy" (Col. 1:18).

In this way, we chase the eternal kingdom of God; but to know exactly what it is, we need to be citizens of the kingdom. The kingdom's glory—the very presence of our Savior—is almost too wonderful to imagine. But God promises that to us.

However, the kingdom of God is also ours in the present moment. We live, work, laugh, cry, struggle, and triumph in a fallen world. But we possess and are possessed by the kingdom of God. It informs our actions, it sets our laws, and it provides its secret rewards and nurtures us in the moment-by-moment. It is both now and coming. Hallelujah!

REFLECTION QUESTIONS

1. How does being poor in spirit differ from having an inferiority complex?

2. Why is it difficult to remain poor in spirit? What can help us?

3. Is poverty of spirit realistic in a competitive world? When should we be able to speak of our qualifications or advocate for ourselves?

MOURNING LIGHT

MATTHEW 5:4

When I was a very young Salvation Army officer, we had in our town an evangelist who had several rescue missions. He was outspoken and seemed to take joy in tweaking the noses of fellow believers and particularly The Salvation Army. When we operated kettles, he had collection buckets a few feet away. Where we had thrift stores, he opened one of his own on the same block. It was irksome to say the least.

One day, he ran his car into some gas pumps because he was driving drunk. He suffered public shame, eventually closing his operations and moving away. When all this was happening, many (myself included) thought he had gotten his comeuppance. But one of the old saints said to me, "People are happy about what happened to him, but it breaks my heart. Here was a fellow believer who fell. We should be mourning for him, praying for him—not rejoicing that he has fallen."

Although we sing and testify about the joy of the Christian life, Jesus said it is not the giddy, but those who mourn who are blessed. Joy and mourning are not mutually exclusive, and the Christian experience includes both. Additionally, mourning in and of itself is not meritorious. Whether due to the death of loved ones, crushing disappointment, or long-term hardship, people feel grief at some point. This emotion is common to the human experience. If you are a believer, you have the comfort of God to depend upon. But this is not the type of mourning Jesus was talking about in the Sermon on the Mount.

So, then, what does it mean to mourn?

We mourn that we ever grieved God. Although we may have sought God's forgiveness and we know that our sins are cast as "far as the east is from the west" (Ps. 103:12), we grieve that we ever brought pain to God's heart by our willful disobedience and rebellion. With that knowledge, we have sorrow for those we hurt by our sin. Although we do not need to dwell on the sins of the past or let their whispers of failure taunt us, we must remember that we are capable of sin, especially when dealing with the faults of others.

We mourn for a world that largely rejects Christ. To listen to the news on TV or radio, or to read it on the internet, is to be assaulted with waves of tragedy, cruelty, and tales of desperation, much of which is directly linked to the sinful condition of humankind. Sometimes it seems as if civilization is about to shake itself apart, to collapse under its faulty structures. We wish, we pray, we campaign for people to turn to Christ as their only hope. And yet we find that too many would rather do anything but *that*. By the testimony of Scripture and by the fruit of our Christian experience, we know what Christ can bring. But still the world largely turns away to plunge itself into its next disaster. We cannot help but mourn.

We mourn the casualties of the war against God. From the Bible's description of Adam and Eve, our first parents, we know that it was God's intention that all people be fed, sheltered, and safe in strong families to live lives full of meaning. Yet in our streets, the legions of homeless form a ragtag parade. Children and other family members who should be nurtured are beaten, demeaned, and sexually abused. Drug and substance abuse is a monster whose appetite never abates, regardless of the souls it devours. Regarded as things instead of human beings, people are trafficked like livestock for slave labor or for perverted sexual desires. Refugees cling to their next-to-nothing bundles as they endure exposure to the elements—a better bargain than seeing their family become grist in the machinery of war. These crimes against creation cause our hearts to mourn. We are driven to action to try to alleviate suffering when we can. And in doing so, we are happy to help, but in drawing closer to the pain, we feel it increasingly in our own hearts. We mourn because injustice exists in a world that a just God created.

Given that, where is the comfort that is promised?

Ultimately, of course, we have the promise of the future. Our Lord "will wipe every tear from their eyes. There will be no more death or mourning or crying or pain, for the old order of things has passed away" (Rev. 21:4). The Bible reminds us that the current state of things is not the ultimate state of things. As bad as it might be, it cannot keep a hold on that which God has claimed for Himself.

In the more immediate moment, we are tasked with doing something about the world in which we live. The blood of Jesus Christ is more powerful than any sin; no soul is beyond His reach. Paul reminded the people of Corinth both what sin was and what they were:

Or do you not know that wrongdoers will not inherit the kingdom of God? Do not be deceived: Neither the sexually immoral nor idolaters nor adulterers nor men who have sex with men, nor thieves nor the greedy nor drunkards nor slanders nor swindlers will inherit the kingdom of God. *And that is what some of you were*. But you were washed, you were sancti-fied, you were justified in the name of the Lord Jesus

Christ and by the Spirit of our God. (1 Cor. 6:9–11, emphasis added)

Every believer is proof that God can do something to change someone. If He can change us, then there is hope for everyone.

Finally, in the name of Christ, we can intercede for those who are in the meat grinder of sin's excess. We do not abandon them to hide ourselves in prayer closets or consultation groups. We have hands, feet, money, and brains. We can find comfort in the giving of comfort.

Praise be to the God and Father of our Lord Jesus Christ, the Father of compassion and the God of all comfort, who comforts us in all our troubles, so that we can comfort those in any trouble with the comfort we ourselves receive from God. For just as we share abundantly in the sufferings of Christ, so also our comfort abounds through Christ. (2 Cor. 1:3–5)

REFLECTION QUESTIONS

1. If Jesus said that those who mourn are blessed, are we wrong to speak of Christian joy? How can we reconcile the two different emotions?

2. How does mourning drive us to action?

3. When was the last time you reached out to comfort someone? Compared to a nonbeliever, in what way do you as a believer comfort another?

3

HUMBLE CONQUERORS

MATTHEW 5:5

Tired of the flattery aimed at him as king of England (AD 994–1035), King Canute moved his throne down to the oceanfront and then commanded the waves not to get him wet. Not surprisingly, he was soon drenched. From that time forward, he never again wore his crown, placing it instead on a statue of the crucified Christ.[1]

During Jesus' time, the idea of humility as a positive personality trait was virtually unknown in the Roman and Greek world. Humility was synonymous with humiliation, such as what a slave faced in everyday life. Instead, the average person was extremely aware of his rights, his position and station in life, his accomplishments, and what he deserved as a result.

Traditional Jewish teaching honored humility, particularly in speaking of a person's standing before God. An example is found in Isaiah 57:15, "The high and lofty one who lives in eternity, the Holy One, says this: 'I live in the high and holy place with those whose spirits are contrite and humble. I restore the crushed spirit of the humble and revive the courage of those with repentant hearts'" (NLT). Quite obviously this attribute did not reach all the hearts of the Jewish believers as evidenced in Jesus' conflicts with the Pharisees and scribes. Nonetheless, unlike the surrounding civilizations, the Scriptures spoke of the need for humility as well as its place in true devotion.

The definition of *meekness* is always a bit elusive. The common thought is that if you think you're humble, you are not. But that defies what Christ is saying here. How can it be that I am to seek something, but never know if I have found it? The problem may not be that we cannot know if we are humble, but that we have defined *humility* incorrectly, at least in the biblical sense.

Dr. Martin Lloyd-Jones has written, "Meekness is essentially a true view of oneself, expressing itself in attitude and conduct with respect to others. It is therefore two things. It is my attitude toward myself; and it is an expression of that in my relationship to others."[2]

Under that definition, we can look at ourselves. Someone has said that an individual is really three persons: that which he thinks he is, that which others think he is, and that which he truly is. Humility means bringing together what a person thinks he is and what he truly is. It is for us to know ourselves and be brutally honest according to the guidance of the Holy Spirit. We own what we are: our talents and abilities, but also our limitations and our failures. Humility includes having a clear self-knowledge of not only our best moments, but also our worst. Scars testify that something didn't go as planned. Humility results from us thinking on those things. There is no task that I am above doing. There is no insult I receive that doesn't include at least a grain of truth or a criticism worth considering.

As Lloyd-Jones has said, humility becomes apparent in how we treat others. Despite our accomplishments, or our self-perceptions in relation to others, or our sense of entitlement, no one owes us anything. As a citizen of my country, I have rights. As a child of God, I do not. Equal rights in the kingdom of God means equal access to serve God and others. There are no protest marches for better treatment, better working conditions, more time off. What we are allowed to do is to freely give to others and humbly not demand things for ourselves.

For the person who possesses meekness, everything is a gift. Any respect I receive is a gift from someone else to me, not something I am owed. Love is not mine to demand, but mine to receive. God does not owe me answers for how things are going in my life. He does not have to answer my prayers as I deem best. Even my salvation is not owed to me. It is a gift of grace, and grace by its very nature is bestowed on someone who doesn't deserve it. And that would be me.

God promises the humble that "they will inherit the earth." In a sense, those who have humble hearts will greet this with genuine surprise. This was a contest they did not enter to win, a possession they did not aspire to have. Because the humble have relinquished their rights, their claims, and their portions, they find their hands are empty enough to receive the gift God places in them.

The earth spoken of here is not the polluted planet of our present day, but the redeemed earth. Here is the new Jerusalem where God will dwell with His people. Reclaimed and restored, it will be the dwelling place of we who have been reclaimed and restored to what we were always meant to be. And when we are there, we will see how foolish it was to grovel for crumbs, to fight over scraps of litter, to stand on the higher step of a stairway that goes nowhere. This is what our Savior wants for His redeemed. But only for those who have emptied themselves of every other possession.

REFLECTION QUESTIONS

1. How would you define *meekness*?

2. Think of someone you regard as meek. What is it about that person that you find admirable? How does that line up with how you live?

4

CRAVING HOLINESS

MATTHEW 5:6

To the contemporaries of Jesus who heard this beatitude, the concepts of hunger and thirst were all too familiar. Even back then, the desert was eating up Israel's traditional borders by increasingly swallowing large land areas in the south. Periodic drought led to inevitable famine. It was all too common for people to realize that, as their crops died in the fields, they would die next.

When drought came and brought famine with it, an already critical situation became dire. Any income from surplus crops evaporated, leaving farmers bereft and cities cut off from food supplies. During drought, the already advancing desert sped up its march to claim what had once been usable farm land. The result was hungry bellies.

During times of severe famine, the Roman government occasionally shared grain with the blighted areas, but they did this as much to garner loyalty as out of compassion. Troublesome regions were simply left to their own devices— and Palestine was decidedly not one of the favored provinces.

To make matters worse, the dry desert heat caused dehydration. Whenever people set out on a journey, they had to carefully calculate their water needs. Miscalculating a water supply when crossing a desert area was far more than an inconvenience; it was effectively a death sentence. When a traveler's water container leaked, he found himself in a major crisis. The Palestinians knew what it meant to be thirsty.

When Jesus spoke of hunger and thirst, His listeners knew the implications in the most extreme sense. The hunger they experienced wasn't like someone whose stomach growls when lunch is fifteen minutes late—it was a fight for life. It is no surprise, then, that the Greek word for hunger is also the word for famine. Thirst was not a my-mouth-is-dry inconvenience but a tongue-shriveling, throat-closing struggle to survive.

When Jesus wanted to communicate the desire for righteousness, He chose terms of intensity: Blessed are those who desire righteousness as much as starving people crave bread or someone with a parched throat desperately thirsts for water.

After Jesus set the stage by speaking about people needing to be poor in spirit, mournful, and meek, He knew that the inevitable next step for the soul was a deep craving to be holy and righteous. Like the starving person seeks food and the thirsty must have water, the person who understands their identity in Christ wants holiness more than anything else. Mere pictures of food and water are empty nourishment; the seeking believer must have the real thing. This desire is not for experiences, for fulfillment, or for excitement. Rather it is a crying need that must find relief.

Dr. James Boice explains, "The meaning is that the one who hungers and thirsts as Christ intends him to hunger and thirst must hunger, not after a partial or imperfect righteousness (either his or God's), but after the whole thing. He must long for a perfect righteousness, and this means, therefore, a righteousness equal to and identical with God's."[1] It should be clearly understood that I am not describing a "good-enough" kind of righteousness, but an all-out pursuit of holiness.

What is the result of this passionate pursuit? "They shall be filled." Isn't it wonderful that Jesus did not say "shall be frustrated" but rather "shall be filled"? The Lord does not implant a thirst that only He can fill without providing for it. Jesus also said, "If you then, though you are evil, know how to give good gifts to your children, how much more will your Father in heaven give the Holy Spirit to those who ask him!" (Luke 11:13). It is the Holy Spirit who sanctifies, who cleanses and fills. He makes us aware of our need for righteousness and helps us believe that this gift is meant for us.

What does this look like? In the words of Sinclair Ferguson, this kind of "righteousness is the situation in which things are what they ought to be."[2] John Wesley added that "the religion we hunger for is the knowledge of God in Christ Jesus."[3] There are many, many facets of the holy life including these mentioned. But all of them are motivated by the right reasons: to love God with pure intention, to seek God and His glory, and to love those He came to seek and to save. Righteousness is holiness at work.

REFLECTION QUESTIONS

1. Have you hungered and thirsted after righteousness? If so, what do these words mean to you now? If not, what is keeping you from knowing this desire for righteousness?

2. Consider this phrase: "Righteousness is holiness at work." How do you experience that?

3. How is your appetite whetted for righteousness?

5

PASSION FOR COMPASSION

MATTHEW 5:7

Years ago, some friends who were vacationing decided to take with them a poor elderly woman from the slums of London's East End. Arriving at the beach, they were surprised when she burst into tears.

"Why in the world are you crying?" the friends asked.

As she pointed to the ocean, she said, "This is the only thing I have ever seen that there was enough of."[1]

When it comes to mercy, you can never have enough.

However, mercy was as much in short supply in Jesus' day as it is for us now. A casual reading of the Gospels, reveals that mercy was too often pushed aside. We see that in Herod's vicious response to Jesus' birth (see Matt. 2:13–23). Those Jewish leaders who did not accept the lordship of Christ evidenced that by their attitudes. The examples continued with the healing of the man with the shriveled hand (see Luke 6:6–11), the man born blind (see John 9), the demoniac (see Mark 5:1–20), and the woman caught in adultery (see John 8:1–11), as well as many other stories. In their quest to be right, misguided leaders often lost sight of mercy in favor of procedure. Procedure in and of itself is not bad—we need it. But people are not meant to be packaged and processed like canned meat.

This lack of mercy was hardly restricted to the Jewish leaders of Jesus' day. Governments throughout the world showed little mercy to anyone. Enemies they captured in battle had no idea whether they would be killed immediately, tortured and then killed, thrown into arenas for blood sport, or end up as slaves. The subjugated people of the Roman Empire were allowed certain freedoms, but those who went beyond the accepted behaviors were not guaranteed a fair hearing much less a just punishment. In the interests of order and control, mercy was virtually nonexistent. Life was harsh. Extending mercy was a luxury that few felt they could afford.

Here again, Jesus put forth an ideal that was counter-cultural. To people who had not seen much mercy modeled or shown to them, Jesus required them to exercise it.

So what does mercy look like?

While grace speaks to our need as sinners, mercy reaches out to people in their misery. Mercy is foundational to how the Christian life is lived. Sir Thomas Elyot rightly observed, "In whom mercy lacketh . . . in him all other virtues be drowned."[2] Mercy coupled with compassion puts feet to the truth of our Christian profession. James 2:16 said bluntly, "As the body without the spirit is dead, so faith without deeds is dead." Throughout the Gospels, Jesus even more graphically commended the merciful and warned those who failed to show it. He summarized the importance of how we treat the less fortunate in these powerful words: "The King will reply, 'Truly I tell you, whatever you did for one of the least of these brothers and sisters of mine, you did for me'" (Matt. 25:40).

We must also remember that mercy differs from pity. Pity often feels the tug at the heart and looks away. Mercy fixes its eyes upon the plight of the one in need and moves to action. Pity acts in the moment. Mercy seeks a permanent change for the better. The difference between the two can be illustrated from an incident in the early history of The Salvation Army.

The founder of The Salvation Army, William Booth, was appalled to see homeless men sleeping under the train trestles in London. Arriving at his office, he called in his son Bramwell, who was his second-in-command. "Did you know that there were men sleeping out each night?"

"Of course," answered Bramwell, "but we have no money to address it."

Not at all satisfied with that answer, the elder Booth thundered, "Do something!" And with that, the first Salvation Army shelter for the homeless soon opened.[3]

As in the other beatitudes, this one comes with a promise to accompany the challenge: Those who show mercy "will be shown mercy."

Perhaps you can remember a time when someone showed you mercy. It may have been after you did something very, very wrong. You had no defense. Your actions were senseless and selfish. You hurt someone, and perhaps upon realizing the damage that you caused, you felt the burden of deep shame not only at what you did, but also that you were even capable of something like that. The offended party did not owe you forgiveness. By all rights, the relationship should have been broken. Even though you were truly sorry for what you did, you did not try to bargain or seek to justify your transgression. You realized that you had no shield of protection; you had nothing left to do, but drop your weapon and hope for mercy.

Maybe you remember a time when you didn't commit a wrong, but when you were in a position of great weakness, or when you suffered a shattering loss. You saw no way to help yourself, let alone a way to pay back anyone who came to your aid. In your helpless state, another's mercy was the only hope you had.

On these occasions, mercy was not something you dispensed from a stronger, superior position. You were the one in the gutter. You stood condemned. How humbling, how sweet it is as the offender to be shown mercy, to be extended a compassionate hand when we are least deserving.

The fact is, we don't only need to show mercy; we need to have mercy shown to us.

REFLECTION QUESTIONS

1. Think of a time when you needed mercy. What happened? What did that do to you?

2. When was the last time someone needed mercy from you? What did you do?

3. Do you agree with the statement: "In whom mercy lacketh . . . in him all other virtues be drowned"? Why or why not?

6

PURE AND CLEAR

MATTHEW 5:8

In 2006, the Barna Group asked Americans whether they considered themselves holy, and reported the results of the survey. Here's what they discovered:

> Three out of four Americans (73%) believe it is possible for someone to become holy regardless of their past. Only half of the adult population (50%), however, said that they knew someone they considered to be holy. That is more than twice as many as those who considered themselves to be holy (21%).
>
> The views of born-again Christians were not much different from the national averages. Among believers, three-quarters (76%) said it is possible for a person to become holy regardless of his or her past. Slightly more than half of the group (55%) said they knew

someone they would describe as holy. And roughly three out of ten Christians (29%) said they themselves were holy, which is marginally more than the national norm.[1]

According to these statistics, 70 percent of average Christian readers come across Jesus' words and think, "He must be talking about someone else." No doubt part of the reason is that when people think of being pure in heart, they envision people like Mother Teresa or some other great saint in the past. How does one measure up to these larger-than-life figures whom always seemed to have an otherworldly demeanor, who spoke in measured and wise tones, and who, by common assent, seemed to walk around with halos adorning their heads? How can common people compete when our lives are filled with temperamental children, difficult coworkers, rude drivers, and not enough money to pay the bills?

What did Jesus mean when He talked about being pure in heart? Did He advise it only for the Mother Teresa types — or did He mean it for the likes of me?

Jesus spoke of being pure in heart as an expected quality of the Christian life, so He obviously meant that this characteristic should be a reality in the life of every believer. While we are glad for the grand examples of the super-saintly, purity of heart is not just for them. It is for you and me.

In a world where all are born into sin, where acting sinful is natural, purity of heart is a markedly different quality than our human nature provides. Martyn Lloyd-Jones shares,

> You can start trying to clean your heart, but at the end of your long life it will be as black as it was at the beginning, perhaps blacker. No! It is God alone who can do it, and, thank God, He has promised to do it. The only way in which we can have a clean heart is for the Holy Spirit to enter into us and to cleanse it for us. Only His indwelling and working within can purify the heart, and He does it by working in us "both to will and to do His good pleasure."[2]

Purity of heart begins with the surrender of our total selves to God. In the experience of salvation, we are born again, forgiven, justified, and transformed from death to life. But as we grow in the Christian life, we find that troublesome habits remain, those intrusive temptations or moments when our spiritual lives are disappointing to others and ourselves. The Christian life too often can be a roller coaster ride from spiritual highs to lows and back up again. As the Holy Spirit moves us toward being conformed to the image of Christ, He implants a desire for something better in us, bidding us to come with a promise that something better is to be had.

We find that even in light of all the glorious things that salvation has brought into our lives, God has something more. He is waiting for us to realize that reality, which is why He lets us struggle and fail in our own efforts. He wants us to release total control to Him. It is the moment when we get down to business with God, beginning with our total surrender. When God purifies the heart of the believer, that person finds that though life must be lived in a sooty, dirty world, purity is preserved in the heart that is undivided toward Him.

Samuel Logan Brengle remarked, "If a water lily could grow in purity and beauty—in startling contrast to the foul waters around and below it—why could not the life of a man made pure and held by God blossom in the midst of a sinful and perverse generation?"[3]

The Sermon on the Mount promises that the pure in heart "will see God." When our focus is on the Lord, not on casting our inner eyes toward a hundred different distractions, we can have clarity of vision. When God does His work, things that were unseen come into view. Suddenly, the microscopic world once invisible to us comes alive, because we have a narrow, magnified focus. We see things we could not have imagined. We begin to see others with the heart of love and compassion with which God sees them. Purity of heart allows us not only to see God in the here and now, but also to prepare our hearts for eternal life in His presence.

REFLECTION QUESTIONS

1. Do you see yourself as pure? Why or why not?

2. If purity is expected in eternity, what does that say about the state of your heart in this moment?

3. What keeps people from being holy?

7

CHILDREN OF
THE PRINCE OF PEACE

MATTHEW 5:9

On the eve of World War II, the prime minister of Great Britain, Neville Chamberlain, met with Adolf Hitler. His intentions were to spare Europe from the carnage that lingered in the memories of those who had experienced the first World War. Chamberlain emerged from that meeting with a peace treaty. Upon his return to England on September 30, 1938, he waved the paper, saying, "I believe we have peace in our time." Less than a year later, Hitler unleashed a blitzkrieg of tanks, aircraft, and shock troops on Poland. World War II had begun.

Although you can find almost a universal desire for peace, history testifies that it remains elusive. At any one time, numerous conflicts rage across the globe. On a smaller scale, clashes exist in homes, churches, schools, workplaces, clubs—almost anywhere groups of people are together for periods of time. Yet we continue to long for peace.

We need to be careful how we define *peace*. Peace is not appeasement, as Chamberlain discovered. Some people will do most anything to avoid confrontation. Too many times confrontation is avoided under the guise of peacemaking, which only results in bullies being allowed to oppress and abuse. These dictators misuse their power, destroying lives by addictions and excesses, all because individuals surrounding the person are afraid to provoke the tyrant. Sidestepping the unpleasant can result in allowing unjust and unrighteous acts to flourish. Ignoring evil was not the kind of peacemaking Jesus was talking about, evidenced by His confrontation with the abusive religious leaders. Peace is always more than the absence of conflict.

Peace, in the biblical sense, includes harmonious relationships, but not at the expense of one party or another, or at the victory of one over the other. The common ground becomes the ingredient for a common peace.

How is such a peace brokered? As we can see from the constant theme that runs throughout the Sermon on the Mount, peace begins with the condition of the heart. Martin Lloyd-Jones commented, "The person who did not have a pure heart, who had a heart which was filled with envy, jealousy and all such horrible things, could never be a peacemaker. The heart must be cleansed before one can possibly make peace."[1]

The peacemaker must be at peace with God. If our own hearts are at war, if we are divided in our allegiance toward God, or ambivalent in our view of sin, we cannot bring to others a peace we do not own ourselves. Whenever we enter into any area where there is conflict, we immediately become aware of the pull toward one way of thinking or another. If our hearts are not pure, our immediate reaction to any view opposing our own is to dig in our heels and search for ways to justify our stance, even though at times we find ourselves battling against a growing conviction that we may need to reconsider. Pigheadedness is not next to godliness.

And we cannot adequately listen if we are too busy talking. Many times, friction is created because someone feels they are not being heard or they are being disregarded. A tremendous amount of conflict can be resolved by an openness to hear what the other person is saying and to empathize with the other person's situation. We will not always be able to give them what they want; most people would like to have more money, but that doesn't mean more money is the answer to their needs. But it is important to understand the circumstances that exist.

Peacemakers must be willing to suffer in pursuit of peace. Sometimes, despite our best efforts, our labors are fruitless. We find that some people are not interested in peace. What might appear to be reasonable and helpful is cast aside, and still worse, the party or parties turn on the one trying to help. Others who seem to be cooperating still have their own ends in mind.

For years, King Saul chased David in the wilderness, not to have a family meeting with his son-in-law, but to destroy him. Time and again, David escaped. On one particular occasion, Saul and his army camped for the night with David and his men nearby. David and a couple of his men sneaked into the camp and took some things of Saul's to leave a sign of their presence, but left without doing the king any harm. Then calling out to the king from a distance, David asked Saul why he continued to pursue him.

Struck by what he was doing, Saul cried out to David, "I have sinned. Come back, David my son. Because you considered my life precious today, I will not try to harm you again. Surely I have acted like a fool and have been terribly wrong" (1 Sam. 26:21).

But David knew that this repentance was shallow. Saul would continue to seek his destruction. Peace could only exist when the two were apart.

Sometimes people's abusive behaviors are so engrained that they continue to be harmful to those they love. Sometimes our desires for peace make us long for instant reconciliation. But for some, peace can only be found by loving someone from a distance.

Peacemakers in the biblical sense are called the "children of God." When the Bible speaks of children in this way, it refers to someone who partakes in the character of the parent.[2] In the same way that God through Christ brought peace to us, we can seek to bring peace to others. And in doing so, we imitate our Father.

REFLECTION QUESTIONS

1. What benefits and/or harm come from appeasement?

2. If you were asked to mediate a conflict, how would you prepare? What strategy would you use when dealing with the parties involved?

3. Do you agree with the idea that for some, peace is only possible when two people are kept apart? Why or why not?

8

THE COST OF
TAKING A STAND

MATTHEW 5:10–12

On February 12, 2015, the Islamic State (ISIL) beheaded twenty-one Coptic Christians. A five-minute video of the execution was released three days later. Reportedly, those Christians were given the opportunity to renounce Christianity but they refused, knowing that martyrdom awaited them.[1] This episode falls in line with a string of targeted killings, which together have made the last one hundred years one of the bloodiest eras of persecution in the history of Christianity.

Citing a report by the Roman Catholic Church, *Newsweek* shared,

The report examined the plight of Christians in China, Egypt, Eritrea, India, Iran, Iraq, Nigeria, North Korea, Pakistan, Saudi Arabia, Sudan, Syria and Turkey over the period lasting from 2015 until 2017. The research showed that in that time, Christians suffered crimes against humanity, and some were hanged or crucified. The report found that Saudi Arabia was the only country where the situation for Christians did not get worse, and that was only because the situation couldn't get any worse than it already was.[2]

Clearly, persecution runs rampant in today's world. However, it's important for us to remember that not everything that happens to Christians is the kind of persecution Jesus was talking about in the Sermon on the Mount.

We aren't suffering for Christ if we are opposed for our political views. We aren't suffering if people don't like us because we are obnoxious or if we have a personality conflict with someone else. Nor do we experience Christian persecution if people dislike us because we are tall, short, thin, overweight, male, female, and so on. This discrimination is upsetting and unfair, but falls into the arena of common humanity. People who are not Christians have to deal with those issues as well.

The persecution Jesus talked about was actions taken against us specifically because we have taken a stand for Him. If we live our lives as Christ asks, we will inevitably come into conflict with those who have different values and beliefs. F. B. Meyer wrote, "The more there is of Christ in us, the more we condemn the world. . . . Jesus Christ is to the ungodly what the sun at noontide is to the diseased eye."[3] We need not seek out persecution; it will come to us on its own.

However, a word of caution: in the Western world, it is commonplace for Christians to be the butt of jokes and derision on TV or other media. That is not pleasant, but if we are honest about it, the media makes fun of nearly everything, including itself. Compared to the severity of persecution presently and over the ages, this kind of thing is hardly worth mentioning. Living fully for Christ will not only place us at odds with the world, but with worldly Christians, or those who give lip service to belief but are Christians in name only.

The world wants a Christian to be an empty-headed, mealy-mouthed, soft-spoken, inoffensive, smiling nebbish who blesses everything and stands against nothing. A toothless Christianity is far more preferable than one that bears a robust witness. Sadly, such witnesses seem to be seen less and less. James Montgomery Boice warned, "The world has become tolerant of us. But we have become far more tolerant of the world."[4]

A holy life is a rebuke to the world. George B. Smith remarked, "A wolf will not worry a painted sheep, a cat will not seize a toy mouse, nor will the world persecute a counterfeit Christian."[5] When the world says, "Eat, drink, and be merry!" the believer says that life is more than food and drink. When the world says, "Live it up!" the believer counters that we live for eternity. When the world says that we deserve to put ourselves first, the believer answers that Christ must be first and the one who orders our lives. And when we live differently—mirroring the life and values of Jesus—we're bound to stick out sooner or later.

When persecution comes, as it will for the true child of God, we must do more than tolerate or endure it. Jesus said that we are to "rejoice and be glad, because great is your reward in heaven" (v. 12). Isn't it strange how something so positive comes from something so evil being directed at us? But persecution for Christ's sake is authentication of what we believe. Faith cannot be known until it is tested any more than steel can prove its strength until it is put under stress. If we rejoice in the moment of trial, we know that this response is the Holy Spirit empowering us for that moment. He is with us!

E. Stanley Jones exulted, "But even if death should come, I am like the bird on the twig of the tree when the storm tries to shake it off. 'All right,' the bird says to itself, 'shake me off. I've still got wings.'"[6] If haters marshal their forces in a charge against us, any pain they inflict is swallowed up in the glory that awaits us.

And how shall we regard those who direct their worst toward us? Jesus said we are to love our enemies (see

Matt. 5:23–47). When we respond to persecution, we must be careful in how we characterize people outside the faith. As believers we are not anticommunist, antigay, antiwhite, anti-anyone. If we take that stance, we put up walls. All men and women are sinners and in need of God's grace. We don't seek to change people's labels, but bring them to a transforming knowledge of Jesus Christ. As John Wesley said, "Let your actions show that you are as genuine in love as they are in hatred."[7]

Finally, we owe our enemies our prayers. They attack because they need the full indwelling of Christ in their lives. They are lost, and unlike those persecuted for righteousness' sake, their futures are beyond bleak.

REFLECTION QUESTIONS

1. Have you ever suffered persecution for the gospel's sake? How did you handle it?

2. Should we intercede on behalf of persecuted Christians or should we allow them to continue their witness?

3. Is the world becoming safer or more dangerous for Christians? Why do you believe that?

9

SAVORY

MATTHEW 5:13–16

Chloride is a highly toxic element that is deadly in gas form. It exists in seawater and in this state can be extremely corrosive. Sodium is an element that attaches itself to other elements to form various chemical compounds. When sodium unites with chloride, it becomes sodium chloride — table salt. That which is otherwise deadly and toxic is rendered useful by being blended with something outside of itself. More than useful, salt is essential to human life. It has multiple uses as a preservative, savory flavoring, and a disinfectant. It has been used in religious ceremonies and as a form of money. The word *salary* is a direct derivative of the Latin word for salt. It represented the Roman soldier's allotment of salt, his "salary."

After outlining the characteristics of the wholehearted believer in the Sermon on the Mount, Jesus then shared with His listeners how they ought to live in the world. As He often did, Jesus chose something very familiar to His listeners to illustrate His point. Salt fit the criteria very well since all homes in Palestine would have had salt.

He told them, "You are the salt of the earth." Note that Jesus did not say that the believer is *like* salt but that he *is* salt. You simply cannot opt out.

But for salt to be effective, it must be used. Salt shakers can be ornate or incredibly simple. Regardless of what they look like, they serve their purpose only when sprinkling salt. As long as salt sits in the shaker or in another container, it serves no purpose. For a believer to be salt, he must perform work out in the world. Although we understand the need for contemplation and reflection, the Christian life was never meant to be lived in isolation. We need to get out there or our beliefs simply don't matter.

To be most effective, salt also needs to be dissolved. In fact, it's best when you can't see it anymore. Although we live in a world that is often hostile to believers and the gospel message, the influence of Christian life and teaching serves as a flavoring throughout Western civilization. In fact, some of the most influential teachings of Mahatma Gandhi were based not on his Hindu theology, but his study of Christianity. When dissolved into a wider discourse, the flavor of Christianity has an influence that too often escapes the notice of the wider world. But it is there because we are there.

One of the best things about salt is that it has always been inexpensive and readily available. After a trip to the grocery store, few people get excited to unpack the salt. There's nothing glamorous about it—yet it is necessary. Quietly and without fanfare, salt does its work. Like salt, most of us lack the kind of talent that will get us on national television or have reporters knocking at our door to get our opinions. Most of us will not have our images adorning coins or the front covers of magazines. But the world needs us, just like our homes need salt.

Usefulness is not defined by popularity. Valuable contributions cannot be calculated by money. By calling us salt, Jesus was saying that in the world, we matter; we have a role that is essential whether or not it is valued.

Before modern refrigeration, the most common way to preserve meat was by salting it. Even with refrigeration, many manufactured products include salt as a preservative as well as a flavoring. We know what happens when preservation fails. If you have ever lost power for a few days and opened a freezer afterward, you know what happens to meat. This world is constantly moving toward decay. Decay is the natural destiny of things. But as the salt of the world, we stall decay by our presence. Imagine if all the Christians were removed. What chaos would result!

But let's not forget that this statement of what we are also comes with a warning: "If salt loses its saltiness, how can it be made salty again? It is no longer good for anything, except to be thrown out and trampled underfoot" (v. 16).

Can a dog quit being a dog? No. Being a dog is its nature. Its owner might train it to do different things, but it remains a dog. If left to its own devices, even the most beautiful purebred will still rummage through the trash like a street hound. A dog's nature is to scavenge, and scavenge it will.

How can salt quit being salty? Inconceivable. Its only reason to exist is to be what it is. If it isn't salt, it must be something else and therefore isn't useful for fulfilling salt's purpose. John Stott shares an interesting note along those lines:

> Dr. David Turk has suggested to me that what was then popularly called "salt" was in fact a white powder (perhaps from around the Dead Sea) which, while containing sodium chloride, also contained much else, since, in those days, there were no refineries. Of this dust the sodium chloride was probably the most soluble component and so the most easily washed out. The residue of white powder still looked like salt, and was doubtless still called salt, but it neither tasted nor acted like salt. It was just road dust.[1]

In a similar way, for the Christian not to have the presence of Christ is an impossible concept. He may look, act, and speak the same, but if we lose Christ, we are but a shadow of grace. If salt loses its essence, it ceases to be. If a believer loses Christ, his salvation is relegated to a past event rather than a present reality.

We are not called the cocaine of the earth to anesthetize people into numbness. We are not called the sugar of the earth to make things go down better. We are called the salt of the earth to do our work in the everyday traffic of life.

REFLECTION QUESTIONS

1. During the week, in what way are you the salt of the earth?

2. In what ways are Christian values influencing our nation?

3. If salt that has lost its saltiness is ineffective, what do you think Jesus meant when He said, "It is no longer good for anything, except to be thrown out and trampled underfoot"?

10

RADIANT

MATTHEW 5:14–16

Leonard Sweet shared the following story in his book, *Aqua Church*: "A missionary home on leave was shopping for a globe of the world to take back to her mission station. The clerk showed her a reasonably priced globe and another one with a light bulb inside. 'This is nicer,' the clerk said, pointing to the illuminated globe, 'but of course, a lighted world costs more.'"[1]

After telling His followers that they were salt, Jesus changed to a different metaphor: light. Again, He did not say they were *like* light but that they *were* light. John Stott noted that in the original Greek, the imperative is especially strong, so it would be correct to read this passage as saying, "you and only you" are the salt and the light of the world.[2]

Science tells us that light is traverse electromagnetic radiation. Light as we know it is 100 percent visible to the human eye. But when light is placed within the context of electromagnetic radiation, the percentage drops to near zero.[3] Light is highly complex, and as we can see by passing it through a prism, light exists as a vast spectrum of colors beyond the white that we think of. Science has found ways to intensify light into more restricted paths so that a laser focuses with such intensity that it can cut through solid objects. To date, researchers have found no limit to the potential intensity of light. Presumably, as science learns more, light can be further and further focused into more concentrated power.

On the other hand, we can know darkness in its absolute. Varying degrees of darkness do not exist. Light dilutes darkness, but we know that if all external light is eliminated, darkness can be so extreme as to render our eyes useless. The Bible repeatedly speaks of people in sin as being in darkness (see Isa. 9:2; Luke 22:53; John 1:5; Acts 26:18; Eph. 5:8, and so on). The only antidote for darkness is light.

Acknowledging that the world outside Christ is in darkness, the Christian stands as light in the world, with Christ as the source of that light. In that role, what is a believer supposed to do?

As light, we are to show what is in the darkness. Anyone who has tried to navigate their bedroom at night without a light knows how dangerous that can be. Even a very faint light will give the outline of what obstacles are in the way, indicate the size of the room, and show the way out. As Christians, we should perform that same function for those dwelling in darkness with the light we cast.

As light, we cannot hide what we are. Jesus compared our role to a city set on a hill. In biblical times, cities contained many small oil lamps that allowed people to discern the presence of the city even from a great distance. Its light made it impossible to conceal it. If we are living for Christ, we not only acknowledge this fact, but also rejoice in it.

Apparently, Jesus was well aware that there were those who wanted to consider their faith a private thing. The world often wants this too, saying, "It is well and good for you to worship as you choose and believe what you want. But keep it to yourself." Unfortunately, too many Christians have accepted the world's standards about illumination instead of the Lord's.

Jesus made an almost comical remark about the way many handle this: "Neither do people light a lamp and put it under a bowl" (v. 15). What's the point of that? Yet even among professed evangelicals, we have too many bowls and not enough lampstands.

This kind of thinking ultimately backfires. We want to seem respectful, but in fact, we are undermining the very faith we say profess. If Christians lived as Christians should, the world's perceptions would be far different. The world's callousness toward Christianity is as much our fault as the devil's work. Our willing retreat behind closed doors, our decision to keep our mouths shut even when we know we should speak, or our desire to be liked by our peers instead of being approved of by God is partially to blame for the mess we are in.

A Christian life genuinely lived is a powerful witness in a dark world. While people around us may not immediately flock to the light we share, when life becomes overwhelming or ceases to make sense to them, they seek out the light bearer. In those moments, we can speak of the hope—the light—that we have in the Light of the World. John Wesley noted, "It is futile to think that we can hide the light, unless we extinguish it. It is impossible to keep our religion from being seen unless we thrust it away!"[4]

The ultimate goal is that "they may see your good deeds and glorify your Father in heaven" (v. 16). Those who hide their light, think life is about them. It never was meant to be. It is about glorifying God with who and what we are because of the change He has made in our hearts. A light is meant to shine. Shine on!

REFLECTION QUESTIONS

1. What do you think about the statement, "As light we are to show what is in the darkness"? How do we show what is in the darkness?

2. Have you ever tried to hide your light? What caused you to do that?

3. How different would your home, workplace, school, or neighborhood be if you allowed your light to shine fully?

11

PURPOSE FULFILLED

MATTHEW 5:17–20

Tony Evans shared, "Lactose intolerance is an allergy to milk. The problem with this condition lies not in the milk but in the biochemical makeup of a person. The flaw lies with the person who ingests the milk. The milk only reveals that fact; it doesn't cause it. The law of God is perfect in every detail. Nothing's wrong with it, but there's something wrong with us."[1]

Jesus' courage to tackle any and all topics is no more clearly proven than in His discussion of the Mosaic law. He waded into this subject with the confidence of a prizefighter facing a sparring opponent. It wasn't like Jesus had a choice. In order for His disciples to understand the kingdom of God, He had to rescue the law from the misapplication and misconception that came with centuries of efforts to "improve" it. It was time for the layers to be peeled away. With the precision of an art restoration expert, Jesus revealed the magnificent masterpiece of the law hidden by the inferior portrait painted over it. The greatness was there, but it was almost impossible to see anymore.

Throughout His ministry, men accused Jesus of destroying the law. But during His ministry's beginning, He clearly stated that He was not opposed to the law at all. What He opposed was the misapplication and the clutter that surrounded it. In their diligence to obey the law, the scribes and Pharisees had made it supreme above all else. That which was intended to lead to an end became the end.

The danger was twofold. Dietrich Bonhoeffer commented:

> It was the error of Israel to put the law in God's place, to make the law their God and their God a law. The disciples were confronted with the opposite danger of denying the law its divinity altogether and divorcing God from his law. Both errors lead to the same result. By confounding God and the law, the Jews were trying to use the law to exploit the Lawgiver: He was swallowed up in the law, and therefore no longer its Lord. By imagining that God and the law could be divorced from one another, the disciples were trying to exploit God by their possession of salvation. In both cases, the gift was confounded with the Giver: God was denied equally, whether it

was with the help of the law, or with the promise of salvation."[2]

Jesus made it clear that He was not to be hemmed in by either of these errors. The law was not an obstacle nor was it a goal. It served a prophetic function. By defining what God wanted, the law gave direction. More than that, the ceremonies and the laws that spoke of outward holiness and obedience found their culmination in the person and work of Jesus Christ. The Passover lamb pointed to the Lamb of God. The approach by blood in the ceremonial law predicted the Son of God's sacrifice. The clean and unclean animals spoke of the importance of what goes into a person and becomes part of him, indicating the way salvation enters and transforms every believer. On and on this symbolism went.

The fulfillment of the law went far beyond obedience to every stroke of a pen. The fulfillment was a person, the perfect One whose life and sacrifice would bring it all into focus. Sinclair B. Ferguson spoke of Christ's death on Calvary as the climax of it all: "There Jesus cried out, 'My God, I am forsaken. Why?' His cry of God-forsakenness, which pierced the darkness of the afternoon of his crucifixion, really says to us: 'This is the penalty of the broken law. This is the meaning of God's law. See how terrible its fulfillment is.'"[3]

Beyond that, Jesus indicated that the law was more than important. Acting like sin is anything less than evil—either by outright teaching or by compromised living (v. 19)—deserves condemnation. Christians do not see the need to continue the civic law of Israel, so they are not bound to stone the adulterer, be fastidious about foods, or worry about sewing two different types of material together in a garment. But the moral law is still in full operation.

In the six scenarios Jesus clearly outlined following the Sermon on the Mount, He illustrated how the law that was given to Moses was just the beginning. A person doesn't need to commit murder to offend God because seething hatred is also wicked. Keeping your hands off another person's spouse is just the beginning of obedience; lusting is not acceptable either. Jesus said the law still mattered, not as the scribes and Pharisees had twisted it, but in its purest form that led to inward change as well as outward observance.

God did not intend the law to be some cumbersome yoke that weighed down His children. As Wesley noted, "Every command in Scripture is really a hidden promise."[4] A heart aligned with the heart of God is in sync. By setting limits, the law declared to us not only what pleases God, but how we might also find ultimate fulfillment for ourselves.

REFLECTION QUESTIONS

1. Paul said that the law was our guardian (see Gal. 3:24–26). In what ways does it teach us?

2. How might someone teach others that God's law is not important? What could be the consequences?

3. If Jesus taught that we must go beyond the outward observance of the law, is He making things more difficult or easier? Why?

THE PRICE OF RAGE

MATTHEW 5:21–26

A *Time* magazine article entitled "America's Anger Is Out of Control" describes the seething anger that was part of the 2016 US presidential election. But the anger neither started nor ended with politics. People in America are angry as a general state of mind. You encounter anger on the highway, in the checkout line, in churches and clubs, between religions and races, and especially on social media. It seems that everyone has a gripe. It takes very little to get tempers to rise to the boiling point. The writer of the article, Jeffrey Kluger, said, "The catch is that rage uncorked becomes rage indulged, and rage indulged becomes rage applauded—and pretty soon anyone with a gripe decides it's OK to crank the dudgeon machine up to eleven."[1] All anger seems justified and worthy of expression to the point that violent acts are commonplace.

Anger is as valid an emotion as love or joy. As such, it has its place and its proper use. When someone attacks my child, my initial emotion is anger, and I rush to my little one's aid. The anger provides the fuel for movement. In a similar way, when the cause of God is attacked unfairly, I am angry because my Lord's honor is assaulted. The initial flash of anger in these and other situations is part of being human. God made us to have a range of emotions for occasions that He knew we would encounter. But, like so many things, there is a proper exercise of anger as well as a sinful one.

The law clearly stated that murder had to be punished. Everyone understood that. But beginning with this account, Jesus began to take the law further than merely outward acts. To wish someone were dead, to fantasize about killing another, or to imagine some great harm coming to another was to mentally and emotionally commit murder. Anger this deep and violent in nature, though it may not lead to the actual act of murder, would affect a person's life. Hating someone that violently is impossible to keep to yourself. The sight of the person, hearing about the person, or thinking about the person causes a surge of hate and anger. Slander, gossip, unjust criticism, insult, and abuse are bound to follow. When an object of anger suffers loss, there is an unholy joy at their misfortune. Often the harm wished is beyond all proportion to the wrongdoing.

Perhaps you remember the old childhood chant, "Sticks and stones may break my bones, but words will never hurt me." But the truth is, words and name-calling are harmful. How many people are injured by verbal abuse suffered in childhood? They include the heartless nickname, the taunts, the cold rejections that even after many years still cause a jab of pain. And the intention of the one who said them was *meant* to be harmful. It is not all in good fun if it is laced with cruelty. Broken bones might actually be more merciful than malicious talk. It is a well-known military practice during war time to use derogatory terms about the enemy so that they are dehumanized and, therefore, easier to kill.

Knowing all this, Jesus put up a fight against anger spilling out into hurtful words. A. B. Bruce helps us understand the weight of the words Jesus used: "*Raca* expresses contempt for a man's head = you stupid!; *more* expresses contempt for his heart and character = you scoundrel!"[2] The Aramaic expression is even harsher than these words. When the word *Raca* is spoken, it sounds like someone clearing his throat before spitting in another person's face, which makes it even more contemptuous.[3]

Hatred has a way of taking over people's lives. We see this through hate groups such as the Ku Klux Klan that find reasons to hate that are beyond any reason. Conspiracies abound, paranoia is rampant, and small incidents that often carry no particular meaning are blown up to be unrecognizable.

But a person doesn't have to be a part of a hate group to be consumed by hate and anger. It can happen with coworkers, fellow students, family members—anyone. That it happens among Christians is tragic in the extreme. The Bible is very clear on this point. The apostle John wrote, "Anyone who hates a brother or sister is a murderer, and you know that no murderer has eternal life residing in him" (1 John 3:15). For a believer to hate another person, especially a fellow Christian, is to make his worship of God null and void. Again, John states bluntly, "Whoever claims to love God yet hates a brother or sister is a liar. For whoever does not love their brother and sister, whom they have seen, cannot love God, whom they have not seen" (1 John 4:20).

Jesus further warned in this teaching that it is better to get things settled lest they backfire. He illustrated His point with a court scenario, telling of a person who pursued legal action against someone else but ended up being tossed into jail by a judge. Jesus was not just offering good legal advice, but issuing a warning about the consequences of living a hate-filled life. In the end, hate causes more self-harm than what it inflicts on another person. The person who hates carries hot coals in his or her shirt. Often the object of his or her hatred is unaware or doesn't care. But still the hatred burns away, embittering and poisoning the life. It ruins a person's spiritual experience, and, if left unchecked, will rob him or her of their salvation.

If you hate someone, you must stop for your own sake. Forgive. Reconcile if possible. Ask for forgiveness from God and the other person. Surrender anger and hate for the blessing that God wants to give you instead.

REFLECTION QUESTIONS

1. Think of a time when someone said something cruel to you. How did it feel? What does that tell you about how we talk to one another?

2. When is anger justified? When is it not?

3. Do you agree that hating someone ruins your spiritual experience? Why or why not?

13

CLEAVING TO ONE

MATTHEW 5:27–32

Speaking about the modern appetite for all things sexual, Tony Evans shared,

Eskimos used to have a way of killing the wolves that they would regularly have to fight in the cold lands. They would put a knife in the ice, blade up. They would take animal blood, put it over the knife, and freeze it. A wolf would smell the blood that was now covering the ice and begin to attempt to lick the blood off. It tasted good to the wolf so the wolf would lick faster and faster and harder and harder, never detecting the sting on its own tongue. All the animal knew was that the blood, unknowingly his own blood, tasted good. The next day the wolf would be dead. It had eaten its own blood because it just couldn't get enough.[1]

Evans went on to say, "We are eating ourselves alive today with sex. We can't get enough."[1] Cable and network television, the internet, magazines, and advertising offer a smorgasbord of lust and twisted morals.

When God created humankind, He made us so that sex was integral to an individual's identity, development, and expression. Beyond propagating the human race, sex serves as the legitimate expression of love between a man and a woman in the context of marriage. It is meant to be contained solely within the marital relationship so that that relationship can be enhanced. When third parties are introduced, it creates something unnatural, resulting in chaos.

When Jesus spoke these words, the people within earshot commonly understood that sex outside marriage was forbidden. We see in the story of the woman caught in adultery that such an offense was often dealt with in the severest terms (see John 8:1–11). But like other areas of the law Jesus addressed, such outward conformity to the law was insufficient. He went a step further: to lust after someone not your spouse, to wish that you could have a sexual relationship with that person, or to give full flight to sexual fantasy, was to commit adultery in the heart.

Because God created us as sexual beings, we are hardwired to notice what is attractive in another. But we are to be more than woodland creatures who respond to the first biological urge that comes into play. The first glance is unavoidable. The second is entirely under our control. The Greek word for *looks at* means "to catch a glimpse out of the corner of one's eye."[2] This is the same as stealing a look. As one author has said, "Deeds of shame are preceded by fantasies of shame, and the inflaming of the imagination by the indiscipline of the eyes."[3]

Not only does lust lead to the possibility of sexual acts but it also leads to the devaluating of one's spouse. When a person lusts, he or she inevitably compares the current object of desire to the one to whom he or she is married. With our culture's constant intrusiveness with sexual content and innuendo, and its flippant attitude about being and remaining married, screening out these toxic messages becomes increasingly difficult.

To counter the potential damage, Jesus spoke in typical literary style for His day by saying, "If your right eye causes you to stumble, gouge it out and throw it away. . . . If your right hand causes you to stumble, cut it off and throw it away. It is better for you to lose one part of your body than for your whole body to go into hell" (vv. 29–30). Some have taken this quite literally and castrated themselves. That is not what Jesus meant at all. It would hardly be a testimony to the transforming and renewing power of the gospel if His followers walked around as voluntary amputees, eunuchs, and eyeless people!

What He was saying was that if we find ourselves likely to be snared in a temptation, it is better to remove ourselves from it no matter how costly that might be. The same is true that an alcoholic should not become a bartender, a gambler should not work at a racetrack, or a sex addict work the counter at Victoria's Secret. Better to give up a job than be snared in temptation. That principle also applies to friendships. Some friends are no good for us and we know it. As hard as it might be to separate from them, it is better to do so than to lose one's salvation. Any situation, relationship, or engagement that pulls us away or places us in temptation is to be avoided at all costs.

In this passage, Jesus also tackled divorce—a very touchy subject even today. We must see His comments in light of the status of women at that time. Divorce was easily obtained, even more so than the present time. Women were dependent upon the men in their lives for their survival. A divorce was more than emotionally devastating—it meant sinking to the lowest kind of existence for women. Dr. Jonathan Pennington notes,

> It would be extremely difficult for a formerly married woman in first-century Judaism to survive economically and socially without being married, thus the assumption is that most divorced women would get remarried. Hence, while initially Jesus' statement

seems to put the burden unfairly on the woman, in fact He is pushing the male perpetrator of an invalid divorce to realize that he is actually the cause of his former wife's adultery, not her, by virtue of forcing her into a remarriage situation when she was wrongly divorced.[4]

Divorce remains a tragedy, a failure, and a broken covenant. Rather than condemn the divorced, we mourn that the relationship they were in came to ruin for whatever reason. As for any penitent person, God compassionately receives and forgives those who have divorced, and in the newness of the Spirit, rejoices in their wholeness found in Him.

REFLECTION QUESTIONS

1. How does pornography relate to what Jesus said about lust?

2. Can you think of anything that was harmful to your spiritual life and needed to be cut out? How did that happen? Is there anything you should cut out now?

3. When is divorce justified? When is it not?

14

VULGARIZING THE SACRED

MATTHEW 5:33–37

The February 6, 2017 edition of *USA Today* reported,

Despite years of battling by the financial industry and a massive change in the way Americans use debit and credit cards, the rate of identity theft soared during 2016, a new report has found. In fact, it hit an all-time high. An estimated 15.4 million consumers were hit with some kind of ID theft last year, according to Javelin Strategy & Research, up from 13.1 million the year before. The report begins ominously: "2016 will be remembered as a banner year for fraudsters, as numerous measures of identity fraud reached new heights." Fraud losses totaled $16 billion, the report found. About 1 in every 16 U.S. adults were victims of ID theft last year (6.15%) — and the incidence rate jumped some 16% year over year.[1]

Identity theft preys upon those who have kept their promises to pay.

When credit is given, it is done on an honor system. The consumer agrees that if he or she is allowed to purchase something on credit then he or she is honor bound to pay for it. When someone signs a credit application, they are in effect declaring an oath to repay their debt. Unfortunately, because enough people have not kept their promises, a whole industry of debt collection has risen to force people to do what they said they would do. No doubt circumstances such as job loss, the loss of family income due to death or divorce, illness, or natural disaster might create issues for people making their payments. But by and large, most credit card companies will work with those individuals as they pass through the crisis. The real problem is with those who live beyond their means or simply use credit with no intention to repay.

In Jesus' day, they did not have credit applications. Instead transactions were largely verbal and were usually accompanied by oaths to emphasize that the parties involved took the transaction seriously. Outside of Judaism, other societies called upon their gods to witness and hold them responsible for what they said. That practice crept into Judaism as well. It should have been enough for people with integrity to promise repayment—but that increasingly was not so.

Today, when people make promises and swear exaggerated oaths to assure us of their sincerity, we often grow suspicious. The expression "I swear on a stack of Bibles" is an example of this. It seems like overkill and makes us suspect that the person is actually not telling us the whole truth.

In Jesus' day, calling upon God in an oath gave the declaration greater weight, but it also placed the person in a precarious position if he or she did not follow through or wasn't telling the truth. As E. Stanley Jones has quoted, "First, God cannot lie, and second, He cannot delegate to you the privilege of lying for Him."[2]

To decrease the risk of breaking a promise sworn before God, the practice in Bible times was to swear by lesser objects rather than calling on God Himself. Jesus cited several of these sorts of oaths. People sometimes swore by heaven, by earth, by Jerusalem, and by their own heads. Christ declared that by swearing oaths on these objects, people were still calling upon God. Heaven is God's throne; earth is His footstool; Jerusalem is the city of the Great King. Someone swearing by their own head was futile, because they had no control over which hairs were black or white (at least in their original state). Beyond that, because God is everywhere, as Bonhoeffer noted, "every word they utter is spoken in His presence, and not only those words which are accompanied by an oath."[3]

Because not keeping an oath was a form of blasphemy against God, the meaning of swearing evolved from declaring an oath to what we now call cussing, itself a derivative of the word *cursing*. Indeed, in ancient days, efforts to call on God in some form were often pronounced in anger. Here is where the use of oaths becomes more than a matter of form but an indication of the heart's condition.

The use of profanity, then, is another sin of speech. We sometimes downplay what we say in the heat of the moment, but God chooses to act in our world through speech. He spoke throughout creation. "God spoke . . . and it was so" (Gen. 1:3–24). Significantly, when John presented Christ in the opening of his Gospel, he chose to refer to Him as the "Word." Even now, we refer to the Lord's guidance as His speaking to us, whether that be through His allowing us to sense His direct communication or through channels like nature, music, literature, and more.

James warned about the perils of being careless in speech:

> The tongue also is a fire, a world of evil among the parts of the body. It corrupts the whole body, sets the whole course of one's life on fire, and is itself set on fire by hell.
>
> All kinds of animals, birds, reptiles and sea creatures are being tamed and have been tamed by mankind,

but no human being can tame the tongue. It is a restless evil, full of deadly poison.

With the tongue we praise our Lord and Father, and with it we curse human beings, who have been made in God's likeness. Out of the same mouth come praise and cursing. My brothers and sisters, this should not be. Can both fresh water and salt water flow from the same spring? My brothers and sisters, can a fig tree bear olives, or a grapevine bear figs? Neither can a salt spring produce fresh water. (James 3:6–12)

We cannot say that words don't matter to God, because Scripture says: "For the mouth speaks what the heart is full of" (Luke 6:45)—and God cares about our hearts.

REFLECTION QUESTIONS

1. If you did not have to sign papers, could you be trusted to honor your financial commitments? How would someone know you would follow through?

2. In what ways does this Scripture speak to you about controlling your speech?

3. Besides using profanity, what other ways can our tongues get us in trouble?

15

SECOND MILE GRACE

MATTHEW 5:38–42

In Papua New Guinea, the tribes have an unwritten law they call "payback." It basically goes, "If you steal one of my chickens, I can steal one of yours." The concept snowballs from there. People commit offenses against each other, and the cycle often stretches over many years, frequently involving injury and death. While serving in that country, a payback drama unfolded before us.

Major Joe Nato, in addition to being a Salvation Army officer, was an elder in one of his tribe's clans in the country's highlands area. Major Joe's clan was involved in payback with another clan that culminated in the death of one of his close relatives. The warring clans gathered for the funeral, each side ready to pounce on the other as soon as the service finished. Major Joe had seen enough. It was expected that when he rose to speak, he would declare that this life would be avenged. Instead, he pleaded in the name of Christ that hostilities cease. As he spoke from his heart, men and women began to weep until it was impossible to hear anyone speak. One by one, men walked to the casket and dropped their weapons by it, forming a heap. That day ended with formerly warring clan members hugging each other and asking for forgiveness.

In His teaching, Jesus referred to the Mosaic law about punishment found in Exodus 21:23–25: "But if there is serious injury, you are to take life for life, eye for eye, tooth for tooth, hand for hand, foot for foot, burn for burn, wound for wound, bruise for bruise." Although many have considered this a justification for retaliation, it was actually a law of restraint. If someone in my family were murdered, I could not demand the slaughter of the murderer's whole family. If I lost my eye, I could not demand the death of the person who caused it. Most importantly, this law was also meant to be used in a judicial setting—not as a justification for individual vengeance.

In contrast to this standard of judgment, Jesus uttered a shocking statement: "Do not resist an evil person" (v. 39). He was still speaking in judicial terms. The word *resist* in the Greek means to take someone to court or give testimony against him.[1] Does this mean that Jesus is opposed to the judicial system? Not at all. The New Testament is quite clear that government authorities are ordained by God (see

John 19:11; Rom. 13:1-2; 1 Peter 2:13). Jesus was not saying that the government should administer justice but that we are not to take matters into our own hands.

Jesus then moved from crime and punishment to injustice in interpersonal relations. The first offense He mentioned is a slap on the cheek. Sinclair Ferguson may help us understand the severity of this act: "Insult it was, of massive proportions, for it was a blow with the back of the hand, something still regarded as grossly offensive in the Near East. The fine for such an insult exceeded the average man's annual wages."[2] In our culture, we still refer to a deliberate insult as "a slap in the face." This action was meant to do more than physically harm a person; it was meant to demean him. In Jesus' day, the only way to handle a slap on the cheek was to take the offender to court, just like we would today in the case of slander or defamation of character.

How did Jesus say that a person should react to such an insult? Turn the other cheek. That response would have been totally unexpected. By turning the other cheek, the power of the insult was null and void. The person refused the insult, offering not defiance but vulnerability. With that, the moral high ground was mounted by gentleness instead of brute force. The effectiveness of this tactic has been seen in history both through Mahatma Gandhi's peaceful revolt against British rule in India and Martin Luther King's leadership of the civil rights movement in the United States. The weapon of nonviolence has no counter weapon. Of course, the offender can continue being violent, but in the end his victory is empty because it was abuse inflicted, not victory won.

This response also underscores a greater truth. As E. Stanley Jones has observed, "The teaching that we are actively to forgive injuries presupposes that the universe goes beyond legal justice and is grounded in love."[3] Jesus demonstrated this love in its perfect sense throughout the ordeal of His betrayal, trial, and crucifixion. His pronouncement on His enemies was not, "Father, blast them for they have wronged Me deeply," but "Father, forgive them, for they do not know what they're doing" (Luke 23:34).

We see the same principle when Jesus described offering someone your coat when they take your shirt away. In those days, a Roman citizen could require a person from a conquered land to carry his load for a mile. The person could not refuse, but neither could he be compelled to go one step farther than the mile.[4] Jesus raised the bar when He told His listeners that they not only had to obey this unjust law, but they were also to do the unexpected. They were to carry the load for a second mile. The believer was under obligation to walk the first mile, but the second mile was done out of love. Imagine the powerful impact this response must have had on the Roman citizens who were accustomed to begrudging obedience, finding now that they were greeted with loving service! The power of this lesson is such that, over 2,000 years later, we still refer to service that goes above and beyond as "going the second mile."

We likely won't be called upon to carry a literal burden for anyone for a mile or two. But we often find ourselves facing unexpected requests for help, interruptions when we are busy, or calls to come alongside others when all we want to do is rest.

Jamie Buckingham faced one such challenge when he was asked to give the refrigerator from his garage to a missionary couple returning home. He heard the Lord say, "Give them the new one. You keep the old one." He struggled with that. He had just paid good money for his new refrigerator. But he knew what love demanded. The new one went to the missionaries.[5]

Jesus closed this teaching by saying, "Give to the one who asks of you, and do not turn away . . ." (v. 42). Jesus, who did not turn away when our need pressed upon Him, challenged us to do the same when the opportunity presents itself.

REFLECTION QUESTIONS

1. Should a Christian ever go to court against another person?

2. Think of a time when you were belittled and insulted. How did you react? How does that compare with the standard Jesus set?

3. When have you gone "the second mile"? What did you think and feel as you were doing it?

16

LOVE WITHOUT LIMITS

MATTHEW 5:43–47

Following a disastrous day of battle for Union forces on December 13, 1863, roughly 7,000 soldiers lay wounded in front of the Confederate lines in Fredericksburg, Virginia. All through the night they moaned and called for help, but no one dared aid them for fear of being shot. Finally, a Confederate soldier named Sergeant Richard Kirkland, a devout Christian from South Carolina, could stand it no longer. He went to Brigadier General Joseph B. Kershaw and asked for permission to take water to the wounded. The general refused but Kirkland insisted.

"Kirkland," the general said, "don't you know that you would get a bullet through your head the moment you stepped over the wall?"

To which Kirkland replied: "Yes, sir. I know that; but if you will let me, I am willing to try it." Kirkland was not allowed to use a white handkerchief to signal a truce but, having gathered all the canteens he could, he went from soldier to soldier handing them life-giving water. Though they were his enemies, Kirkland saw them as people in need. For his actions, he was called "The Angel of Marye's Heights."[1]

Loving our family members is natural. The bonds of affection and commitment are strengthened over time by shared experiences and goals, the natural result of living in a small community of humans who must learn to give, take, receive, and sacrifice for each other. Families are the basic units of civilization and have a profound influence on individuals. The general rule is that if something is wrong with the family, it will affect all the family members as well. Love is best modeled and learned within families. This principle is true regardless of station in life, country, ethnic group or tribe, and language. It's also true regardless of how much chaos or prosperity exists outside the home. For someone to love another family member is expected and natural. Loving those who join our circle of friends and our extended family members, is one of life's great joys. This expectation is universal.

While affirming the rightness of these kinds of love, Jesus also drilled deeper by insisting that we love our enemies. He did not define whom He meant by enemies, or what their motivations were. Sometimes enemies are those of another nation who hate people just because of where they come from. Most often, though, we make enemies in the course of living. At some point, a person who was perhaps close to us drifted away, and their affection turned into intense hatred. Or sometimes, those who previously had neutral feelings toward us catalogued reasons to dislike us and allowed those feelings to blossom into hate.

We know someone is an enemy when our presence, our actions, or simply our reputations inflame their feelings of revulsion. They wish us harm and may even be motivated to cause that harm. They rejoice in our misfortunes and celebrate in our failures. Yet Jesus told us to love people like that.

In speaking of loving people, Jesus indicated that we are to love with a stronger love than they can hate. The Greek word He used is the familiar term *agapé,* that unselfish and all-giving love that characterized Jesus' love for His disciples; He expected that same love back from them in return. Those who practice agapé will act in the best interests of their enemies.[2] Dietrich Bonhoeffer wrote, "No sacrifice which a lover would make for his beloved is too great for us to make for our enemy."[3]

When we demonstrate this kind of love, it can make a profound impact. On October 2, 2006, in Lancaster County, Pennsylvania, a lone gunman by the name of Charles Carl Roberts, entered a one-room Amish schoolhouse. Taking hostages, he shot eight out of ten girls, killing five of them before killing himself. The small community of peace-loving Amish were shocked at the senselessness of this act, which contrasted sharply with the pacifism that marks Amish beliefs. But their response afterward embodied grace:

> On the day of the shooting, a grandfather of one of the murdered Amish girls was heard warning some young relatives not to hate the killer, saying, "We must not think evil of this man." Another Amish father noted, "He had a mother and a wife and a soul and now he's standing before a just God." Jack Meyer, a member of the Brethren community living near the Amish in Lancaster County, explained: "I don't think there's anybody here that wants to do anything but forgive and not only reach out to those who have suffered a loss in that way but to reach out to the family of the man who committed these acts."
>
> A Roberts family spokesman said an Amish neighbor comforted the gunman's family hours after the shooting and extended forgiveness to them. Amish community members visited and comforted Roberts' widow, parents, and parents-in-law. One Amish man held Roberts' sobbing father in his arms, reportedly for as long as an hour, to comfort him. The Amish have also set up a charitable fund for the family of the shooter. About 30 members of the

Amish community attended Roberts' funeral, and Marie Roberts, the widow of the killer, was one of the few outsiders invited to the funeral of one of the victims.[4]

Several times, Paul reminded believers that they were the enemies of God before they were reconciled to Christ. Our sin is harmful not only to us and the people around us but also, whether we know it or not, to God. But He loves us. "God demonstrates his own love for us in this: While we were still sinners, Christ died for us" (Rom. 5:8). Should we not love our enemies as Christ has loved us?

REFLECTION QUESTIONS

1. Think about an enemy you have now or had in the past. What caused this enmity? Is there anything you did to contribute to the ill feeling?

2. What is the hardest thing about loving an enemy?

3. Place yourself in the position of the Amish community the author described in this devotional. Could you have acted as they did? Why or why not?

17

PERFECT IN THE FATHER'S EYES

MATTHEW 5:48

As a very nervous new parent, I went with my wife to take our newborn for her first physical examination by the pediatrician. We were still giddy about having this new life in our home, but also so very nervous about doing everything right, making sure we protected her from any physical danger, and providing for her needs. We had read and talked with other parents, but nothing was as reassuring as the conclusion of our little girl's examination when the doctor said, "She is a perfect baby." I am quite sure he said that to a lot of people, but to us, no words could have been more thrilling in that moment.

When he said "perfect," did he mean that she was fully mature? That she was ready to walk? That she could go to school next week? Of course not. What he was saying was that all the organs in that tiny body were working as they should. That her mental acuity was where it should be at her age. All her appendages were where they should be, and she evidenced good nutrition. "Perfect" did not mean there was no improvement ahead. It simply meant that she was a complete and healthy infant.

Many have stumbled over Jesus' words, "Be perfect, therefore, as your heavenly Father is perfect." It sounds like Jesus is requiring us to do and to be what is impossible this side of heaven. Those outside of the Wesleyan-Arminian camp dismiss this verse and its meaning all too readily because it cannot fit into their theology. But the question is not one of theology, but of considering what Jesus meant.

The Greek word for perfect is *telios*, which is best translated as "complete." When the King James Version of the Bible was translated, that was what *perfect* meant, but over time, the definition grew closer to "absolutely flawless" or "unable to be improved upon." When we take this more modern definition and couple it with Scripture's demand that we be like our heavenly Father—whose perfection in all His attributes is beyond our comprehension—we are dwarfed by the thought of it. But viewing perfection as "being complete" is another thing. God is complete in Himself, and in some ways, though not all, we can be complete as well.

The fall of humankind resulted in an inherited sinful nature, which essentially means we are born as damaged goods. We then inflict even more damage on ourselves through our willful sinning. Imagine we are each a steel pitcher with a manufacturing defect that causes it to lean to one side. Someone takes their frustrations out on the pitcher by banging on it with a hammer. It is still recognized as a pitcher, but a person wouldn't want to use it to serve guests.

Through salvation, the Lord cleans up that pitcher and bangs out some of the dents. The pitcher still has scars from misuse, but we also begin to see a remarkable difference. Now we can fill that pitcher with water—right to the top. Though still an imperfect pitcher, it can be full of clean water, and serve a purpose.

In holiness, God fills us with His Holy Spirit so that, though we may be scarred from our life choices, the effects of our sinful nature and our natural limitations, we can be complete by serving as the vessels we are. We still are not perfect in the world's eyes, but we render what service we can with the abilities we have. There is a wholeness about us even with the defects that afflict us. We can fulfil the Great Commandments to "love the Lord your God with all your heart and with all your soul and with all your mind" and to "love your neighbor as yourself" (Matt. 22:36–39).

Holiness is not a static state. We pass through the stages of life, and with each one, we face new challenges. What was monumentally important for me at sixteen years old, is vastly different from what is monumentally important at sixty. As long as I live, I am constantly changing, and the way the Lord relates to me and I to Him, changes as well. Each life stage calls forth new questions and requires us to redefine ourselves. Likewise, the experience of holiness also finds new channels of expression and application in our lives.

We continue to experience growth as God leads us forward. Although God performs an enormous work when He saves and then sanctifies us, we would be overwhelmed if He revealed all the changes He intended to make in us over time. We are flawed creatures, and God hammers out our defects one at a time. Just when we feel at peace, God shows us an area that we need to address, a place where He wishes to lead us, or a service that previously escaped our notice. Our hearts are no longer content to remain as they are. Before God revealed those new realities to us, we were not disobedient because we were unaware of them. But once God moves us in a new direction, we must follow His Spirit along that path.

In being perfect like our heavenly Father, we gain His viewpoint. We do not love only those who are lovely, we do not seek to be among only those who are just like us. Like God, we should reach across societal barriers, even if we feel the pain that comes with stretching. We should understand that doing the right thing is never isolated, but is a step along the road of seeking to bless others.

Christ was absolutely perfect by all definitions, yet He was despised, rejected, hated, mocked, and crucified. We who are His children cannot expect to be treated better than our Lord. We might wish that if we love as Christ loved, the world would welcome us. Sadly, life is not so. But we love anyway. We serve anyway. We live holy lives anyway. Following Christ was never about popularity, but about wholeness.

REFLECTION QUESTIONS

1. Do you believe that holiness is what Jesus meant when He said we are to "be perfect like the heavenly Father is perfect"? Why or why not?

2. Knowing we are scarred from past sin, how can we serve the Lord fully with the defects we still have?

3. How can someone be complete yet still need to grow?

18

ONLY FOR THE FATHER'S EYES

MATTHEW 6:1–8

When the Duke of Wellington was still known as Arthur Wellsley, he brokered negotiations following a key battle while serving with the British army in colonial India. An emissary from an Indian ruler who hoped to gain territory, pressed Wellsley for information, but could not get him to talk. Finally, the emissary offered him a bribe that was the equivalent of £50,000. "Can you keep a secret?" asked Wellsley. "Yes, indeed," was the emissary's reply. "So can I," Wellsley responded.[1]

In this section of the Sermon on the Mount, Jesus continued to drill down into the hearts of the people. Here He mentioned two spiritual disciplines: almsgiving and praying. Both are good things that enhance the spiritual life. Both can bring us closer to God. Both can also be derailed so that even when they are performed flawlessly, they can fail miserably. Giving that bankrupts the giver may still fall short. Prayers that people quote through the ages can end up going nowhere. The action a human performs is not necessarily the action God approves.

In Jesus' day, Jews held their religious leaders in the highest esteem. But the danger with fawning over and exalting someone—both then and now—is that the person may be tempted to keep a little glory for himself. An unholy competition can surface as leaders vie to outdo each other for a bit more adulation.

In Jesus' day, blowing a trumpet indicated an urgent matter, most often during a financial crisis. Shops were quickly closed as the pious raced to the scene of disaster to offer their gifts. Their running signaled to everyone who saw them that they wanted to be first to make their commitments. And if they were not the first, they gave more to compensate.[2]

Trumpets were also used in the days when water was in short supply in Palestine. Some religious leaders ordered that trumpets would be sounded to announce water distribution. Pious people stood by proudly, acting as benefactors to those in need, showing the crowds the depth of their mercy and good works.[3] These were good deeds, no doubt. The modern equivalent is the presentation of an oversized check to a charity with cameras rolling and the crowd applauding. The fact that gifts are good is not in question.

The question we should ask is, who really benefits — the giver or the ones receiving the gifts?

Jesus used a very strong word to describe those who have divided motives behind their good works: hypocrites. The word *hypocrite* is from Greek theater. Originally it meant someone who was an orator, but then it evolved to refer to actors. In those days, actors wore masks, which means a hypocrite was someone who literally portrayed himself as one thing, but was in fact something else. Eventually the word became associated with showiness and the desire to be on the big stage to display good works. Those who gave in a manner that glorified themselves were rebuked for their hypocrisy.[4]

Jesus also rebuked those who gloried in their public prayers. He wasn't saying that public prayer is wrong. Oftentimes heartfelt or well-considered prayers capture what we wish we could say or remind us of God's greatness and goodness. Sincere prayer is not the target here.

The prayers Jesus rebuked were akin to oratory, grand speeches meant to make others comment, "That man must be close to God! Listen to how beautiful his prayers are!" Hypocrites uttered those prayers with one eye closed and the other open to see who was impressed. They loved listening to the gasps of wonder at the grandiose phrases they used. Perhaps through all that rhetoric, some of their listeners were drawn close to God — but if that happened, it was likely in spite of the showy prayers rather than because of them. God isn't impressed by vocabulary or theatrics in the performance of duties. Like Dorothy and her friends in *The Wizard of Oz*, God knows what is going on behind the curtain.

Jesus said that those who give gifts and those who pray for show "have received their reward in full." The term He used was a commercial one used for transactions. It literally meant, "to receive a sum in full and give a receipt for it."[5] Those sorts of hypocrites received acclaim in the moment because of their gifts and prayers, but that's it. Eventually the momentary glory evaporated and left nothing of lasting value behind.

Instead of acting this way, Jesus instructed His followers to perform their acts in secret. God is everywhere, and what His children do does not escape His notice. When we perform good deeds as acts of worship, as we should, then the fact that God knows about them is quite enough. While we can't always pray and give to the poor in complete secrecy, our focus should be on how we honor God rather than on what people think of us.

Jesus reassures us that, "The Father knows what you need before you ask" (v. 8). We need not shout, because God is not deaf. We need not approach Him with fear, because He desires to give us what we need. We need not feel ashamed before Him, because He regards us with the riches of His love. He knows us, our needs, and how best to proceed.

REFLECTION QUESTIONS

1. Some Christians are famous. Is it wrong that they are? Why or why not?

2. How should we handle praise for our work for God?

3. Jesus said that those who seek not to be noticed for their actions of charity and their prayers will receive their reward (vv. 4, 6). What do you think the reward is?

19

THE MODEL PRAYER: ADORATION

MATTHEW 6:9–10

Tony Evans has observed, "For many of us, prayer is like the National Anthem before a football game. It gets the game started, but simply has no connection with what's happening on the field. It's a courtesy."[1] Perhaps too many believers share this sentiment, but the Bible portrays something quite different. A view more aligned with the Scriptures is found in the song lyrics that say,

> Prayer is the soul's sincere desire
> Uttered or unexpressed,
> The motion of a hidden fire
> That trembles in the breast.[2]

Prayer is a mystery. It was in Jesus' day and it is now. We often go to prayer with the best of intentions, but end up in imaginary conversations with people we anticipate meeting that day, or making grocery lists, etc. Our minds operate independently of what we want, like when we slip a car into neutral and find that it rolls in a direction of its own choosing. No wonder that good Jewish boys who were raised in synagogues since birth approached Jesus with the request, "Lord, teach us to pray" (Luke 11:1).

Knowing all this, Jesus shared the model prayer—often called "The Lord's Prayer"—with us. The Lord's Prayer guides us not only through content, but also provides a path that is useful to us as we go before the Lord.

Each phrase of this prayer gives us a glimpse into how we, too, can approach God. In the first part, Christ focused on adoration. We should stand before our glorious God not with hands outstretched to receive, but with hearts overflowing to offer Him worship, praise, and heartfelt gratitude for who He is. Our adoration acknowledges His claims, His glory, and the ideals of His kingdom.

Our Father in heaven. This beautiful opening was unthinkably familiar in Jesus' day. Christ used the Aramaic word *Abba*, a term of greatest intimacy, akin to our word *daddy*.[3] In calling God "Father," Jesus was not only bringing people closer to God in their thinking, but also revealing something about God's character that had been lost in the ostentatious prayers of religious leaders. Like a father who joyfully picks up his child and sets him on his lap, the heavenly Father welcomes the intimacy of His children who approach Him.

At the same time, Jesus also reminded people of God's transcendence. God has no beginning and no end, occupies a space that we will presently hear about, and dwells where our best imaginings cannot take us. We are locked into a single realm, but God moves freely in dimensions unknowable to anyone but Himself. Years cannot bind Him, distances cannot restrict His movement, and the volume of the universe cannot hide even one fact from His knowledge. The phrase "Our Father in heaven" recognizes that God is both near at hand and present where we cannot be.

Hallowed be Your name. If we can catch our breath after thinking just for a few moments of God's everywhereness, His all-knowingness, His boundless stance above time, and His limitless power, we know that His name should be more than reverenced. If we came physically face-to-face with God, we would not be like giddy autograph seekers, but would rather be overwhelmed by the magnitude of His being, His holiness, and His glory. Our reaction would be more like Isaiah's, who could only see how unfit he was when ushered into the presence of God (see Isa. 6:1–8). Holy is His name because He is altogether holy.

Your kingdom come, Your will be done, on earth as it is in heaven. This next part is a reminder that God has a claim on this world of ours. Yes, the devil has been trying to compete with the Almighty, but he will never be more than a squatter. God owns the title deed to the earth. On His appointed day, He will reassert His rights to what is already His.

The kingdom will come. We whose hearts are God's, long for that day. But the kingdom fulfilled on earth is also the kingdom fulfilled in us. When God comes to reign upon this earth, we will not need to hunger and thirst after righteousness; we will not have to be peacemakers. We will not be concerned with fulfilling the law, with lust or divorce, with our hatred or hatred that others direct toward us. Sideways or biased justice or pretentious prayers will no longer be issues. Our dear Lord will set it all right. The justice we crave, the honor we seek for our Master, and the hope that propels us forward, will all reside in the New Jerusalem.

This is not just something that will eventually happen. God's kingdom is at work now. Each God-honoring church is an outpost in enemy territory. Each Spirit-filled Christian is a soldier in the battle. To be sure, our enemy continues to fire volleys, and he has sent spies among us who undermine our unity, distract us from our priorities, and continue to batter and abuse us. But the kingdom shall come, on earth as it is in heaven. That prayer is more than wishful thinking. It describes our destiny.

The kingdom to come is more real than anything we now call reality. This earth will disappear like a mist, but the kingdom of God will endure beyond the last flame that sputters on the sun. And that is something for which we can forever adore Him.

REFLECTION QUESTIONS

1. How is our Father both very close, but also highly exalted?

2. How can we treat God's name as hallowed?

3. The kingdom of God is both a present reality and a promised future. How do we see God's kingdom at work now? How will that differ after the Lord has returned?

20

THE MODEL PRAYER: PETITION

MATTHEW 6:11–13

Abraham Lincoln, who loved a good story, particularly enjoyed the one about two women who were discussing him and the president of the Confederacy, Jefferson Davis. "I think Jefferson will succeed because he is a praying man," said the first lady.

"But so is Abraham a praying man," countered the other.

"Yes," the first one replied, "but the Lord will think that Abraham is joking."[1]

Two major themes are at the heart of the second half of the Lord's Prayer: prayer should be taken seriously, and God takes the prayers of His people seriously. After honoring God and ascribing Him glory in the first half, the second half centers on the petitions of children of God. No matter how well off we may think we are, we always remain in a state of need. No one has arrived; no one has gotten to the place where self-sufficiency has replaced what only God can give. The stronger we grow in Christ, the more we know we need Him—and here's how we should ask.

Give us this day our daily bread. No doubt when the people heard Jesus speak of daily bread, they were reminded of the miracle of the manna, the daily ration the Israelites received while they wandered in the wilderness. As you can see in Jesus' discussion with some people following the feeding of the 5,000 (see John 6:30–32), the Jewish people seemed to carry an expectation that when the Messiah came, He would also provide bread in this fashion.

However, the request for "daily bread" refers to more than just a constant supply of groceries. Bread was the staple food for most people in the Roman Empire; as such, it represents the most basic needs. Besides nourishment, bread represents strength and absence of debilitating want. D. A. Carson shared, "The word translated 'daily' occurs very rarely in Greek. In fact, it is found with one hundred percent certainty only in this prayer."[2] The word *daily*, then, reminds us of our constant need to trust God in each moment, to know that whatever happens next, He will supply the daily bread of His sustenance.

God is more than interested in the full range of our need. Commissioner Samuel Logan Brengle wrote,

Nothing that is of interest to us is too small to interest Him. . . . [People] think God is interested only in the big things, but the same God that made the flaming suns and mighty worlds made the tiny insect, fashioned the lenses of the eye and painted with brightest colors its dainty wings. He is interested in the little quite as much as in the great. Therefore, we may bring everything to Him in prayer.[3]

We must remember that bread represents our necessities, not our craving for luxuries. The kingdom of God is not likely to be advanced by shiny cars or the latest video game systems. We may sometimes receive these things, but it isn't right to ask God for baubles that indulge our selfishness, especially when so much want exists in the world.

And forgive us our debts, as we have forgiven our debtors. Our needs extend beyond physical and emotional requirements. Throughout life, we all experience failure. Misunderstandings occur. Feelings get hurt, and sometimes people aim deliberate acts of malice against us. To live among people is to risk harming them, even if that harm is unintentional. Even the holiest person can be caught off guard by temptation or slip into sin occasionally. We naturally want to nurse our wounds, plot revenge, and then find ways to carry out those schemes. Even if we don't commit outward acts, our revenge fantasies can feed wounded spirits over an inordinate length of time. But people who are truly repentant will own their sin and humbly ask God for forgiveness.

In Jesus' day, forgiveness was meted out sparingly. Families carried grudges for generations. People remembered how other countries had wronged them hundreds of years before, and those memories provided fuel for smoldering fires of hate. Peter thought he was being generous when he asked Jesus if forgiving a person seven times was enough. He was shocked by Jesus' response that it was only the beginning (see Matt. 18:21–22).

It is surprising how even Christians too often want a measure of grace shown to them that they are not willing to show to others. As seen in this prayer, Christ will have none of that. We need both to forgive as well as be forgiven.

And lead us not into temptation, but deliver us from the evil one. Temptation is not the same as sinning. Christ Himself was tempted, so we know that being lured toward something wrong is not the same as committing a sin. Continuing in that direction is another story. But if we seek to live a holy life, we should acknowledge that we would rather not be placed in the position of even thinking about doing something that displeases God.

The King James Version of Scripture translates a word in this passage to mean "evil," but modern Bible versions more accurately translate it as "the evil one." Although it has become somewhat unfashionable in some Christian circles to talk about the devil, the Bible treats him as a real personality whose activities are counter to the interests of God. In praying for deliverance from the evil one, we acknowledge that Satan can harm us, and we admit that unless the Lord protects us, we can fall under Satan's influence. The devil is delighted when we commit one of two errors: give him too much credit or ignore him altogether. Jesus did not obsess about the devil, but He did recognize the harm Satan can cause to unsuspecting or careless souls. We should follow suit.

REFLECTION QUESTIONS

1. How would you define your "daily bread"?

2. What can you do if someone refuses to forgive you? Is forgiveness something that you owe to another person?

3. If there is one temptation from which you would especially like to be delivered, what is it? How would you like to see God help you in this area?

21

THE MODEL PRAYER: PATH OF FORGIVENESS

MATTHEW 6:14–15

The late Senator Mark Hatfield shared the story of President James Garfield who, six months after his election, was shot in the back in an assassination attempt. A doctor attempted to probe the wound in search of the bullet, but failed to locate it. He tried again with a silver-tipped probe, but again could not locate the bullet. Over and over teams dug into the wound to try to remove the bullet, but all the attempts were unsuccessful. Finally, Alexander Graham Bell, inventor of the telephone, also sought the bullet, but without success. The president hung on for a couple more months before he died. But it wasn't from the bullet. It was from an infection caused by all the probing.[1]

In the same way, an offense can be painful and unjust, but an inability to forgive can infect a person's soul far worse than the original wrong. Forgiveness is so important that Jesus revisited it in this passage of Scripture. No religion emphasizes forgiveness as much as Christianity. Even in this post-Christian era that has descended like a cloud over the Western World, Christian values remain integrated into the culture. One of those values is forgiveness.

One of the clearest demonstrations of forgiveness occurred after World War II when the Marshall Plan was instituted to rebuild countries devastated by the war, including countries that had fought against the Allies. In fascist nations, rubble was cleared from the streets, infrastructure was repaired and expanded, homes were rebuilt, and economies were resurrected for the very people who'd taken up arms and wreaked havoc across the world. In Japan, cities blighted by bombing were carefully rebuilt, industry was reestablished, and the country was healed by an infusion of aid and expertise. Forgiveness rebuilt a broken world.

Because forgiveness is a cultural value, Americans struggle to understand the Middle East as well as other parts of the world not affected by Christianity. In most places, forgiveness is not considered to be important, so wrongs that occurred centuries ago are remembered and eventually avenged. No doubt forgiveness occurs on an individual basis in those places, but it isn't so common in the affairs of nations. As shown by the Marshall Plan cited earlier, and by recent warming relations with Vietnam,

Americans generally feel that peaceful outlooks should follow war. In cultures that don't value forgiveness, however, defeat is only one more offense to foster and to remember until vengeance is rendered.

Forgiveness is important for both healthy bodies and souls. Grudges can have negative short-term and long-term effects, including headaches, digestion problems, insomnia, increased anxiety, depression, high blood pressure, skin problems (such as eczema), heart problems, and stroke.[2] To "forgive and forget" is not always easy, but, in time, forgiveness brings healing.

Jesus reminded His listeners that an unforgiving spirit damages the spiritual relationship between a believer and God. That's why He said, "if you do not forgive others their sins, your Father will not forgive your sins" (v. 15).

Our Christian experience is far more than a private matter between us and God. The Bible repeatedly makes it clear that a social element exists in our life in Christ. Loving God means loving others, looking out for their interests, and seeking their good even when they act hatefully toward us. There is no exception to this rule. We are not allowed the luxury of withholding our blessings from any person. Quite the contrary. We are *required* to reach out to them.

Jesus warned elsewhere of the consequences of not caring for others:

I was a stranger and you did not invite me in, I needed clothes and you did not clothe me, I was sick and in prison and you did not look after me. They also will answer, "Lord, when did we see you hungry or thirsty or a stranger or needing clothes or sick or in prison, and did not help you?" He will reply, "Truly I tell you, whatever you did not do for one of the least of these, you did not do for me." (Matt. 25:43–45)

Eternal destiny hangs in the balance based on how we treat others, including whether or not we forgive them. This reality is nothing to trifle with.

Forgiveness often must come without justice. In a perfect world, we would always forgive others and, when necessary, they would forgive us. In reality, that doesn't always happen. But regardless of whether others show us grace, we are required to.

Forgiving others does not mean we offer ourselves as an outlet for their violence. It's not sinful to separate ourselves from dangerous offenders. The sin is to withhold forgiveness. We can forgive people who continue to be aggressive, belligerent, or even abusive. However, we may need to distance ourselves from that person for self-protection—as in the case of domestic violence.

We are still forgiven even if the other person continues to remind us of our wrong. As vexing as that is, we must realize that we do not have the ability to force others to forgive us. We can handle only our responsibility. We should forgive even when forgiveness is withheld from us. We should reach out in love even when others spit in our face.

When we forgive, we not only loose ourselves from hatred's burden, but we become more like our Lord who forgave us despite the many wrongs we commit against Him. God's forgiveness begets our forgiveness—and our forgiveness is proof of His life in us.

REFLECTION QUESTIONS

1. Have you struggled to forgive someone? Where are you now in that process?

2. Do you see forgiveness as an American cultural value? Is that value changing?

3. Why does being unforgiving endanger our salvation?

22

NOT SO FAST

MATTHEW 6:16–18

Fasting represents one of the strongest forms of self-denial. Commissioner Samuel Logan Brengle wrote,

> We deny ourselves when we voluntarily give up that which we like, and which we might lawfully keep. And I have no doubt that God often allows us luxuries and abundance, not that we may consume them upon ourselves, but rather that we may deny ourselves joyfully for His dear sake, and the sake of the needy ones about us.[1]

For millennia, fasting has been an important spiritual discipline, reaching far beyond the Judeo-Christian religious experience. Although this practice normally centers around denying oneself food for a specified period, fasting can involve more than that. In our day, fasts can include a break from technology. For many, food is easier to give up than that an electronic device. However, much of the teachings about fasting from food can also apply to the subject of self-denial as a whole.

Fasting's main purpose doesn't involve losing weight or weaning oneself away from something addictive. Rather, fasting is a way to clear the mind and heart so you can become more focused in seeking after God. It should be accompanied by a spirit of repentance and humility. You may find fasting useful when asking God to reveal His will, when seeking repentance for some past sin, and when declaring your need for His mercy and grace. We don't fast to seek God's approval—God already extends that to us through His grace. But fasting is a useful tool to help us ask God for clarity, vision, and sensitivity to His Spirit.

From the text of Matthew 6:16–18, we know Jesus expected His followers to fast. He said, "*When* you fast . . ." (v. 16). Fasting had long been part of the Jewish calendar to commemorate such events as the Day of Atonement and to remember tragedies such as the destruction of the temple. Jewish leaders also called fasts when their community came under peril, as described in the book of Esther (see Est. 4:15–16).[2]

In this part of the Sermon on the Mount, Jesus focused more on the "how" of fasting than the "why." The Pharisees fasted not only to fulfil the requirements of the law, but also to make it part of their weekly routines. Some Pharisees were genuinely pious, but others saw fasting as a way to show off their superiority. Jesus mentioned this when He said they looked "somber . . . they disfigure their faces to show others they are fasting" (v. 16).

Perhaps these Pharisees also stumbled around from weakness, holding their stomachs and dropping in a heap as they reached their destinations. When offered food, we can imagine them waving it off, as they moaned above a whisper, "I cannot. I am fasting before the Lord." Who would not be moved by such a display of (supposed) holiness. Jesus' depiction of the Pharisees' response to fasting seems to have had a touch of humor as He related a scene that His listeners had seen many times and about which they likely scoffed in secret.

As with the showy almsgiving and prayers outlined earlier in the chapter (vv. 1–8), Jesus condemned the fruit of the Pharisees' labors, saying: "They have received their reward in full" (v. 16). The Pharisees impressed others, but that is where their reward ended.

Jesus also outlined how His followers were to fast. He said, "When you fast, put oil on your head and wash your face, so that it will not be obvious to others that you are fasting." (v. 17). Carl G. Vaught offered a helpful explanation of this verse: "Anointing the head with oil was the classical Hebrew symbol for the presence of God's Spirit within, and washing was the symbol for the cleansed soul that was the precondition of the transformed life."[3]

It is interesting that, using an exercise which typically represented repentance and humility before God, Jesus called for His disciples to present a public face of rejoicing and spiritual peace to the world. Is it wrong, then, to show grief for personal sin or mourning for the sins of a nation, such as Daniel and Nehemiah's lamentations? We all face times when we must share the burdens of our hearts with others, including the grief we feel when God's work is compromised or under attack.

The critical difference between appropriate spiritual mourning and the hypocritical prayers of the Pharisees lies in the focus. What the Pharisees practiced was spiritual theater that exalted them over their fellows who weren't fasting; it made them headliners in their own show of spiritual performance. Theirs was a "tears on demand" kind of religion that did not glorify God, but focused on themselves.

If we choose self-denial or fasting in response to our grief and legitimate concerns for God's work, then our focus is not on us but on God's glory. As a body of believers, our grief should move us to act. We should not purposefully draw attention to ourselves, however. Fasting cannot be replaced by a feast of self-gratification.

In one city where I served, I recall a religious leader going on a hunger strike for a cause for which we both were working. The resulting media attention, while mentioning his cause, focused more on his act of self-denial. It was strange to see his ordeal chronicled on local television and in the newspaper. Though his original purpose was laudable, he soon became caught up in the media's focus on him.

Proper self-denial should be done for Christ's sake — for an audience of one. No one else need be involved. That One will reward us according to His righteous standards.

REFLECTION QUESTIONS

1. Have you ever fasted? If so, why? If not, why not?

2. Describe a personal experience with someone who displayed religious piety for show. What observations did you make?

3. Jesus said that those who fast correctly and in secret will be rewarded by the Father in heaven. How might God reward them?

23

TREASURE OF THE HEART

MATTHEW 6:19–24

In 1995, the US Congress battled over a controversial tax cut bill. At the center of it was a provision to crack down on wealthy Americans who renounce their citizenship to avoid paying taxes. One politician called them "Benedict Arnold billionaires." Money changed their priorities and their loyalties.[1]

How believers handle money has been a challenge since the beginning. Even more so in our day than in Jesus' day, money is integral to almost all facets of life. In ancient times, through bartering and subsistence farming, a family could scrape by with very little cash. But in today's economy, we constantly deal with money we never actually see, as funds are transferred electronically in and out of our bank accounts, through credit cards, and by scores of other means. To unplug entirely from this system is nigh impossible.

Identity thieves raise havoc with security, heartlessly drain bank accounts, and ruin credit, which makes every day carry a measure of financial risk. And with electronic stock trading, pension funds can experience dramatic losses in a matter of hours. Today's financial climate and systems make it all the more difficult not to think about money.

In Jesus' day, it was also difficult for the wealthy not to be concerned. If they kept their wealth in their homes, they risked the very things Jesus warned about: "moths and vermin destroy, and . . . thieves break in and steal" (v. 19). In those days, the temples offered a degree of security by also serving as storage vaults for the wealthy. But that made them special targets for marauding bandits or invading armies that looted temples not only for the objects of worship made from precious metals, but also for the wealth in the vaults. To have wealth was to have something to worry about.

While the Lord would not have told His followers to be careless with money, He did not want to see people so concerned about it that it took their focus away from what was of eternal value. He counseled people to "store up . . . treasures in heaven. . . . For where your treasure is, your heart will be also" (vv. 20–21). The problem with money is that, although we hope it will serve us, it often becomes our master. We see this clearly regarding the issue of stewardship.

When my wife and I served in Jamaica as divisional leaders for The Salvation Army (comparable to district superintendents), we often held congregational meetings. Like their North American counterparts, Jamaicans were not great givers to their corps (churches). I recall frequently asking, "Do you believe that God can revive this community so that the worst sinners get saved?"

"Hallelujah! Glory to God! Yes, Major!" they responded.

"Do you believe that God can heal the worst disease and cause the lame to leap?" I asked.

"Hallelujah! Glory to God!" they cried out again.

"And do you believe that if you give God 10 percent of your income He can take care of all your needs?" I asked.

Soft mumble.

That's the rub. Even if we have little, we sometimes feel we must hold on to what we have without considering that God gave it to us in the first place. Poor people can become just as focused and obsessed with money as any billionaire.

The fixation on money and material possessions can blind us. That is why Jesus continued this passage by talking about spiritual vision. He said, "The eye is the lamp of the body. If your eyes are healthy, your whole body will be full of light. But if your eyes are unhealthy, your whole body will be full of darkness. If then the light within you is darkness, how great is that darkness!" (vv. 22–23).

The word translated in the NIV as *healthy* was used in the Greek version of the Old Testament to mean "singleness of purpose, undivided loyalty."[2] In contrast with that definition, the word that the NIV translated as *unhealthy* literally means "folded over."[3] The idea of "folded over" could be understood as "double-minded." One evidence of a holy heart is that a person wholeheartedly gives themself to the Lord, with single-minded devotion. The carnal Christian tries to be a part of two worlds going in different directions. The double-mindedness that results from this confuses them, stunts their growth, and clouds their spiritual insight and vision.

Jesus emphasized this matter by saying that no one can serve two masters. You will hate the one and love the other. You cannot serve both God and mammon (money) (v. 24). *Mammon* originally meant "something which is entrusted," but the word evolved to mean "that which a man trusts."[4] In time, people equated mammon with money since that was the most common representation of mammon.

As mammon (money) grows increasingly important to a person, it demands more of that person's loyalty and attention. Their focus moves away from the Lord. How many of us have taken a job that required us to work on Sundays, and, because we pursued money, our own affection toward the Lord cooled? While many vital service professions require work on Sunday, most jobs do not. Or how often do we feel tempted to keep our monthly tithe rather than give it to the church because we either fear we won't have enough to live on or we want to purchase something beyond our budget? Do we willingly choose the lure of money over our commitment to and faith in God?

Francis Bacon said that "money is a great servant but a bad master."[5] You will love one and hate the other. For the Christian, the wrong attitude toward money can eat the soul.

REFLECTION QUESTIONS

1. Think of a time when you have been deeply concerned about money. Where did your trust in God come into play?

2. What is your attitude toward tithing? How is it a measurement of your faith in God?

3. How can you keep a balanced view of money and material things?

24

FIRST THING

MATTHEW 6:25–34

An old legend tells of a day when Death was headed toward a city. A man stopped Death to ask what he was going to do. "I plan to kill 10,000 people in that city over there."

The man cried out, "That's terrible!"

Death replied, "Well, that is my job. It's what I do."

The man ran into the city to warn people. He went from place to place to tell them of Death's plan. At the end of the day he met Death again. "I thought you were going to kill 10,000 people but 70,000 people died. What happened?"

Death answered, "I only killed 10,000. Worry and fear killed the others."[1]

After Jesus taught the importance of having the right perspective on money and material possessions, He described the Father's care for His children. He talked about this during a time when there was great uncertainty in the world. Famine and drought could happen at any time. Armed revolts often swept away the innocent, and those who survived got caught in the crossfire of inevitable retaliations. The Jews were a conquered people, and they knew that genocide was a reality that stronger nations could inflict on weaker ones. Medical science at that time didn't understand how diseases affected the body, much less how diseases spread, which resulted in plagues that ushered tens of thousands of souls into eternity within short periods of time. Infant and child deaths were also common, and many young mothers breathed their last during childbirth. Those times were perilous.

In addition to all these dangers, some people just have personalities that predispose them to worrying. They fear what is there or what could be there. They hear about catastrophes and know that something similar could happen to them. Perhaps they quite wisely prepare for the worst, but even when that is done, they worry about things for which no preparation can be made. After all, where in the world are you truly safe from an asteroid? Every disaster movie makes it clear that unless you're the heroine, you don't stand a chance.

Whether the reasons for fear and worry seem to be real or not, they are very real to the person who experiences them. Jesus' words provide a balm to anxious souls.

First, He told His listeners to have the right perspective. One of the great problems with worry and anxiety is that they fuel themselves, making the initial concerns seem impossibly huge. Remember the last time you stubbed your toe? The other 99 percent of your body was pain free, but at that moment, your toe grabbed all the attention. Jesus gently said, "Is not life more than food, and the body more than clothes?" (v. 25). Embrace the perspective that there is often more right than wrong and that though you face threats, you also have people and things upon which you can fully depend. Most of all, remember that God is faithful.

Next, Jesus reminded His listeners that birds and flowers live their lives free of worry. Why? Because the heavenly Father looks after their interests. We have a bird feeder in our backyard. My grandchildren love to go out with me to put seed in the feeder and then sprinkle some on the ground for the squirrels. But occasionally we get busy and forget, or we go away for a few days and the seed runs out. We have yet to find starved birds on the ground or emaciated squirrels hanging from the trees. They find something else to eat because the Father has already looked after their interests.

Jesus went on to say that those who do not believe in Him are concerned about these things, the essentials, but the children of God should not be. Christ comforted His listeners by reminding them, "Your heavenly Father knows that you need them" (v. 32). He was saying that you belong to the One who furnished the power to light all the stars in the universe. His design is stamped on galaxies and tiny atoms. The sky that spreads over you diffuses sunlight to protect you and carries clouds to provide you with water. It's not difficult for God to put a shirt on your back or food on your table. He knows what we need. If for some reason we don't get it, we probably didn't need it at all. Or perhaps, like when Elijah left the sheltering brook of Cherith (see 1 Kings 17:7–9), God needs to move you along to somewhere else.

The child of God shouldn't constantly be concerned about things. As Christians, we shouldn't be seekers of things but seekers of Him. "Seek first his kingdom and his righteousness . . ." (v. 33). Keep Him ever before you. Look after the interests of the kingdom of God, and the King will make sure you have what you need.

Deep in God's heart, He has reasons why He wants us to carry out His will, despite the fact that He is self-sufficient. He doesn't really need us. But He has chosen to involve us in His work—not to distract us from what is important but to help us focus on what is.

Finally, Jesus reminded His listeners that a person cannot do a blessed thing about unknown future events. We all have our hands full dealing with the troubles of today, and the same will be true when the new day dawns. Although you can plan for tomorrow, your plans cannot happen until you get there. Be encouraged, though—the Father is already there. He already knows what you will need then just as He knows what you will need five minutes from now.

REFLECTION QUESTIONS

1. What worries you the most? How do you find relief from the worry?

2. Is it ever helpful to tell someone not to worry? Why or why not? What should you say?

3. What's the difference between trusting God and failing to prepare?

25

EYE OF THE HYPOCRITE

MATTHEW 7:1–6

In our publications for The Salvation Army, we include a puzzle page. By far, the favorite feature is "Spot the Difference." We use two seemingly identical pictures, but one is altered: something is taken out, an object's color is changed, or something new is placed in the photo. People enjoy those puzzles as a mental challenge because they allow them to exercise their God-given abilities to be mismatch detectors. We are hardwired to notice the hair out of place, the wrinkle in the shirt, or the lint on the skirt. God gave us this gift to help us with far more serious survival issues. Our ancestors had to notice when something was amiss as they trekked through forests, looking for signs that indicated danger was near. Similarly, a military commander watching a battle unfold needs to notice when things change so he knows when to move his troops around.

That skill can have a negative side to it, however, especially when it impacts our relationships with others. Sometimes people don't use the skill as God intended. Examples include bosses who find only faults, parents who criticize every behavior, or spouses who overlook good qualities to point out failings. After Jesus spoke about our relationship with the Father, He returned to our relationship with others. We can never stray too far from the social expression of holiness. Faith is at work in all areas of life.

Jesus instructed, "Do not judge, or you too will be judged" (v. 1). He added that we will be judged by the same measure with which we judge others. If you have been tactful, considerate, and kindly, you can expect tact, consideration, and kindness. But if you have been angry, cruel, or unfair, you can expect to receive that treatment back in full measure. We may think that we point out others' shortcomings with our criticisms, but really they reveal our inner flaws. As E. Stanley Jones has said, "When religious people begin backsliding, they begin backbiting."[1]

Oftentimes a critical spirit forms because a person is dealing with his own sense of inadequacy. Rather than improving themselves or going before the Lord to seek Him for what He can do in their lives, people try to bring others down, not just to their level, but to a place beneath them. It's like trying to stand taller by building a tower of carcasses.

A level of deceit is involved. The worst motives, the most critical judgment, is leveled toward the one condemned. Exaggeration degenerates to outright deceit as evil motives are imagined about the other party—fictitious conversations taking on the status of historical fact. Grace may be there for others, they feel, but this object of scorn is beyond any hope. If something unquestionably good is done by the one, they disdain it and quickly explain it away.

Jesus used a ludicrous example to illustrate the folly of such a mind-set: "Why do you look at the speck of sawdust in your brother's eye and pay no attention to the plank in your own eye?" (v. 3). The word for *speck* in the NIV is correctly translated to mean a small bit of sawdust or chaff. The word for *plank* is more accurately translated as a wooden rafter or a log.[2]

A person with a hypercritical attitude expends as much energy as is needed to collect evidence against and catalogue the faults of the person they hate. This can be far more serious than any wrongs the person actually committed. When a speck of sawdust is there, we don't need to use a club for a scalpel. Our first duty is to deal with our own dark hearts and address our own faults before going on a crusade to eradicate the faults of others.

That said, we must still recognize the difference between being judgmental and using good judgment. Jesus illustrated that in graphic terms, saying: "Do not give dogs what is sacred; do not throw your pearls to pigs. If you do, they may trample them under their feet, and turn and tear you to pieces" (v. 6).

Although dogs have a high place in our culture as pets and companions, it was not so during Jesus' day. Dogs were not highly regarded in Scripture, being numbered among the unclean animals. They are mentioned forty times in the Bible, none of the references complimentary. Considered to be a nuisance, they were most often running through the streets in packs where they scavenged for food and frequently attacked people and other animals.[3]

Pigs were worse. An abomination to the Jews, pigs were not only filthy in their normal existence, but could also be violent. The Palestinian domestic pig most likely was a descendant of the European wild boar, a particularly aggressive and vicious creature.[4] In Jewish culture, nothing was worthwhile about swine.

If we are not supposed to judge, what can Jesus mean by referring to some people as being akin to dogs and pigs? How do we know who they are if we don't make a judgment?

Again, we are not to lack judgment, but to employ it without a sense of superiority or condemnation, knowing that someday we will have to answer to God for our sins. If you've ever dealt with someone poisoned by their own attitude, you know that despite trying to reason with them, they will not listen. They may even attack you if you dare to defend someone in front of them. We should note that pearls are valuable to us, but to pigs, they are meaningless. The same is true regarding embittered souls: all they do is attack. In essence, Jesus was saying not to waste time with people who viciously assault others, lest you become the next victim.

We must tread softly and be constantly aware that we are made of frail dust and will eventually answer to the Almighty God for our wayward attitudes and thoughts. Sometimes we must offer others criticism or instruction, but we ought to provide it in the most tender way possible, as if we were on the receiving end.

REFLECTION QUESTIONS

1. What's the difference between being judgmental and having good judgment?

2. If we are naturally inclined to find differences, how do we make sure it is for a positive result instead of a negative one?

3. How can we reach someone who has become bitter?

26

PERSISTENCE IN PRAYER

MATTHEW 7:7–12

A few years ago, a bar was scheduled to open in a town that previously had been dry. Believers at one church began to pray that the bar would not open. Soon after, lightning struck the building where the bar was to be located and it burned to the ground. The bar owner sued the church, claiming that because of its prayers, they were responsible for his loss. The church's lawyer countered that the church wasn't responsible. The judge said, "No matter how this case comes out, one thing is clear. The tavern owner believes in prayer and the Christians do not."[1]

As Jesus neared the end of His sermon, He returned once again to the subject of prayer. He outlined how life in the kingdom of God differs from what His listeners thought it was. The religious leaders especially felt they had it all figured out, but, if they'd listened to Jesus' words, they would have realized that they had missed an awful lot. To be poor in spirit, meek, merciful, and a peacemaker is challenging indeed. To be salt and light is a round-the-clock duty. The religious leaders hadn't anticipated Jesus' higher standards for sexual purity, treatment of enemies, turning the other cheek, giving, prayer, and fasting. How could they possibly do all that without God's help? That was precisely the point. They couldn't—and neither can we.

They must have felt quite relieved when Jesus told them that they could go to the Father for assistance: "Ask and it will be given to you; seek and you will find; knock and the door will be opened to you" (v. 7). The Greek forms of the verbs more accurately read, "Ask and keep on asking. . . . seek and keep on seeking, . . . knock and keep on knocking."[2] Persistence is the main idea. It may take time for our requests to be answered. Additionally, we must remember that we aren't seeking a one-time gift. We are never self-sufficient; our lives are sustained only by the grace of God through His Holy Spirit. I needed Him in the past, I need Him now, and I will always need Him.

Some have taken this verse to mean that whatever they ask for, they will get. Those who preach the prosperity gospel have propagated this view; they promise that individuals who follow a prescribed formula can rest assured that God is turning the keys to the kingdom over to them so they can have whatever they want.

Other, more sincere souls plead to God for legitimate needs that they keenly feel He must give to them. After all, it is proper to bring before the Lord prayers for the seriously ill, for much-needed money, or for relief from some condition. And the petitioners know what is needed: health for the sick, money for the needy, intervention for the condition, etc. They go to the Lord with prayers, and they think they know exactly how He should answer them, complete with the timetable He needs to keep. They say, "Just endorse my plan, dear Lord."

People who offer those sorts of prayers think that doing so is right. After all, doesn't God say, "For everyone who asks receives; . . . and to the one who knocks, the door will be opened"? (v. 8). Receives, yes. The door does open for them. But what is received is not necessarily what is asked for, and the door that opens may lead to another way altogether.

When my wife and I were raising our children, we assigned them chores appropriate to their ages. We calculated a monetary value for each chore and explained to them that we would not just hand out money. If they did their chores, they could control how much money they got. Our oldest son accepted this system begrudgingly, always feeling he should just be able to come and get what he wanted when he wanted it. One of the chores he did not like was making his bed, but he did it because he liked getting the money for it. Finally, he moved away from home and started earning his own living.

But during one particularly chaotic period of his life, when it seemed nothing was working out for him, he told his mother, "Every morning I make my bed. Other things in my life may be messed up, but at least I can make my bed. I have control over that. Thank you for making me learn to do it." As a child he wanted the money with no responsibility, but it was the responsibility that ended up being more valuable than the few cents we gave him.

Many times, we realize with the benefit of hindsight that if God had given us what we thought we needed, it would have been disastrous. Perhaps something much better took place because God put us where we really needed to be. Unlike television episodes that tie everything up neatly at the end, not everything is that obvious in life. Sometimes we clearly see God at work in a situation, but other times our questions go unanswered. This doesn't mean God wasn't at work; it means that, even if He'd told us what He was doing, we wouldn't have understood it.

I don't have a clue regarding how most parts of my car function, but I'm still content to let it carry me where I need to go. Likewise, we cannot always discern God's workings, but we can be sure that He will do what is needed. Even if we don't get answers on this side of heaven, we should trust God anyway. As William McGill has said, "The value of persistent prayer is not that He will hear us . . . but that we will hear Him."[3]

Jesus reminded His listeners of the heavenly Father's goodness by asking what earthly father would give a hungry child a stone or a snake instead of a fish. Jesus declared, "How much more will your Father in heaven give good gifts to those who ask him!" (v. 11). John R. W. Stott said, "The reason has to do with us, not with Him; the question is not whether He is ready to give, but whether we are ready to receive."[4]

Our God may not always supply what we want, but He will supply all that we need.

REFLECTION QUESTIONS

1. How does what Jesus said in the Sermon on the Mount affect the content of your prayers?

2. Think about a time when God did not give you what you asked for, but you later understood why. What does that teach you about prayer?

3. When someone is praying desperately for something, how can we counsel them to accept the answer or non-answer that God gives?

27

ROUTE TO RIGHTEOUSNESS

MATTHEW 7:13–14

In 2011, the Barna Group did a survey of Americans regarding universalism—the idea that all people will go to heaven regardless of their beliefs. They also asked for their views about pluralism—the idea that there are multiple paths to heaven through different religions. As one might expect, increasing numbers of Americans accepted both beliefs, including evangelical Christians.

Looking specifically at universalism, 40 percent of Americans agreed with this statement: "All people will experience the same outcome after death, regardless of their religious beliefs." A surprising 25 percent of American evangelicals also agreed. That same percentage of American evangelicals also agreed with the idea that "all people are eventually saved or accepted by God, no matter what they do, because He loves all people He has created."

When faced with the question of pluralism, 59 percent of Americans agreed with the statement, "Christians and Muslims worship the same God even though they have different names and beliefs regarding God." Among evangelicals, 40 percent also accepted that as true.[1]

Contrast this murky theology with what Jesus said: "Enter through the narrow gate. For wide is the gate and broad is the road that leads to destruction, and many enter through it. But small is the gate and narrow the road that leads to life, and only a few find it" (vv. 13–14). Clearly, large numbers of people experience a disconnect between what they believe and what the Bible says.

When Jesus began His ministry, most of the Jews held the view that as God's chosen people, they were guaranteed a place in the heavenly kingdom. The Gentiles, if willing to become Jews, were allowed this same privilege. Gentile believers who did not fully convert to Judaism were called "God fearers," and the Jews viewed them sympathetically as well. Overall, though, Jews had very narrow beliefs, and very few attempted to win Gentiles over to their faith.

It became abundantly clear to the early church that God intended salvation to be for all people. The conversion of Cornelius with its accompanying miraculous revelation (see Acts 10), confirmed that God intended to offer His salvation to all, even Gentiles. A church council soon after confirmed that the Gentiles did not have to convert to Judaism as a condition of salvation (see Acts 15). But even though a universal call of salvation went out to all people, the conditions of salvation remained narrow. Jesus said quite plainly, "I am the way and the truth and the life. No one comes to the Father except through me" (John 14:6). Similar language is found throughout the New Testament, making it clear that salvation could only be had by believing in Christ as Savior accompanied by repentance from sin.

Jesus knew that following this standard would be difficult. It meant that those brought up in the Jewish faith were now being told their beliefs were incomplete and that they had to approach God in the same manner as the despised Gentiles. The exclusiveness of Christ as the means of salvation was a stumbling block to them (see 1 Cor. 1:23; 1 Peter 2:8). That has not changed over the centuries.

Saying that the way to heaven is narrow flies in the face of us who live in a democratic society that insists on equality of all. But we need to realize that the kingdom of God is not a democracy. We do not elect God; we do not campaign for a change in the laws He has ordained. Unlike our public officials, God is not accountable to us.

Not only is the way in narrow, but the only other way, broad though it may be, "leads to destruction" (v. 13). A third way doesn't exist. There is no hybrid path. You can choose only one or the other.

This "destruction" has often been interpreted as hell. We seldom speak of hell these days because of our reluctance to scare people into the kingdom. But the Bible is not bashful at all in speaking of it. None of Scripture's allusions to hell are pleasant (see Ezek. 18:20; Matt. 13:50, 25:46; 2 Thess. 1:9; 2 Peter 2:4; Rev. 21:8). None lend credence to the ridiculous notion of those who say, "I want to go to hell because all my friends will be there."

No one in their right mind wants to think of people tormented for eternity. We may often experience regret that hell is the destiny for those who reject Christ as Savior. That reality makes it even more urgent for Christians to be salt and light, so that others might find Him.

Jesus also made it clear that if you are going to be a disciple, don't expect to be speeding along on a superhighway. The way is narrow, confining. The disciplines are demanding. The expectations are high. Living the holy life as outlined in the Sermon on the Mount means that we are on a different path than our neighbors, many in our family, and our friends at work or in school. The words of the old gospel song come to mind:

> I traveled down a lonely road
> And no one seemed to care;
> The burden on my weary back
> Had bowed me to despair,

I oft complained to Jesus
How folks were treating me,
And then I heard Him say so tenderly,
"My feet were also weary,
Upon the Calvary road;
The cross became so heavy,
I fell beneath the load,
Be faithful weary pilgrim,
The morning I can see,
Just lift your cross and follow close to Me."

"I work so hard for Jesus"
I often boast and say,
"I've sacrificed a lot of things
To walk the narrow way,
I gave up fame and fortune,
I'm worth a lot to Thee,"
And then I hear Him gently say to me,
"I left the throne of glory
And counted it but loss,
My hands were nailed in anger
Upon a cruel cross,
But now we'll make the journey
With your hand safe in Mine,
So lift your cross and follow close to Me."

Oh, Jesus if I die upon a foreign field someday,
"Twould be no more than love demands
No less could I repay,
"No greater love hath mortal man
Than for a friend to die"
These are the words He gently spoke to me,
"If just a cup of water
I place within your hand
Then just a cup of water
Is all that I demand,"
But if by death to living
They can Thy glory see,
I'll take my cross and follow close to Thee.[2]

REFLECTION QUESTIONS

1. Given what Jesus says in today's devotional, how are you fulfilling your responsibility to witness?

2. How would you answer someone who says that it doesn't matter what a person believes to enter heaven?

3. With the path of discipleship being narrow, how does that affect how you live?

28

FRUIT INSPECTION

MATTHEW 7:15-20

Jim Jones headed the People's Temple located in San Francisco where he was also active in local community affairs. In the early 1970s, Jones and many of his followers relocated to Jonestown, Guyana. When human rights abuses were alleged against them, Congressman Leo Ryan led a delegation to investigate. He and others in his party were murdered when they attempted to take off with defectors among Jones' followers. Knowing that these murders would not go unpunished, Jones led nine hundred and eighteen of his followers in a mass murder-suicide that shocked the world. Of the victims, three hundred and four were children, who were given cyanide in a fruit-flavored drink. After his death, it was revealed that he had committed widespread sexual abuse of men, women, and children.[1] Jim Jones was the textbook definition of a false prophet.

The problem of false prophets is nothing new. Jeremiah frequently had confrontations with false prophets who tried to counter his strong message of repentance (see Jer. 23:16; 28:17). Through Moses, God gave a test for determining whether someone was a false prophet: "If what a prophet proclaims in the name of the Lord does not take place or come true, that is a message the Lord has not spoken. That prophet has spoken presumptuously, so do not be alarmed" (Deut. 18:22). In fulfillment of Jesus' warning, the New Testament is filled with numerous warnings about false prophets by Paul (see Acts 20:28–30; 2 Tim. 4:3–4), by Peter (see 2 Peter 3:14–18), and by John (see 1 John 4:1–6).

The Jewish nation struggled against idolatry for much of its history, as recorded in the Old Testament. But one of the benefits of the Babylonian captivity was that idolatry was never again a major issue for the Jewish nation. However, religious leaders continued to prey on them—as well as on the Christian church—by subverting the message of the gospel in both what it said and how it is practiced.

The methodology false prophets employed in biblical times is similar to the strategies deceivers use today. Some of those deceivers may have started as sincere people, but something happened to change that; some thought or temptation took hold of them until they drifted away from the true faith. For example, Jim Jones received a number of community awards while he worked in San Francisco. Like

Jones, many false prophets initially look like everyone else: they talk and act like other believers and may be considered role models. As Jesus said, "They come to you in sheep's clothing" (v. 15).

The false prophet does not usually establish himself with some shocking teaching. Rather, he starts with the familiar, finds common ground with his followers, then slowly leads them in another direction. If you have ever swam in the ocean than you know what it is like to look up and see that you have unknowingly drifted down the beach from where you got into the water. The current moved you. False prophets are similar in how they introduce a shift in beliefs. Later, they often claim to have received some special revelation or discovered some teaching that was lost over time or suppressed by the church. Sometimes he or she introduces additional "scriptures" or secret teachings that either supplement the Bible or reveal special insights no one else has. Note this, however: false prophets cannot go very far without changing fundamental teachings about the character of Jesus Christ, the Trinity, and the Bible.

Soon after the false prophet introduces new teaching, that teaching often leads to misconduct among the prophet and his followers; misconduct that contradicts scriptural standards. Many of these issues revolve around either money or sex. Jesus warned, "Every good tree bears good fruit, but a bad tree bears bad fruit. A good tree cannot bear bad fruit and a bad tree cannot bear good fruit. Every tree that does not bear good fruit is cut down and thrown into the fire. Thus, by their fruit you will recognize them" (vv. 17–20). While a wolf may be able to hide in disguise among sheep, as John Stott said, "No tree can hide its identity for long. Sooner or later it betrays itself—by its fruit."[2] You can't get peaches from a cherry tree nor can you get apples from a mango tree. The fruit reveals the tree's nature.

Why would someone even want to be a false prophet?

No doubt some people feel they have stumbled on some great truth. Even as they try to form their new theology, however, they find they must disregard evidence that opposes their viewpoint and reinterpret Scripture that might call their teaching into question.

More likely the false teacher finds it intoxicating to be adored by his followers. Those who closely associate with the one who introduces "new" truths find themselves in a more privileged position than others. They treat any opposition like proof that they must be right; others must be jealously trying to regain ground lost to the new movement. Thus, opposition fans the flames of loyalty, the very thing which feeds the false prophet's movement. This loyalty also allows the false prophet to encroach upon those closest to him. His followers must give increasing amounts of money to the cause. The prophet solicits sexual favors from his followers as proof of allegiance or as a love offering.

As the false prophet becomes addicted to adulation, his followers grow increasingly addicted to him.

Sadly, church history is full of tales about false teachers. Some quickly rise and fall while others establish more permanent work that goes beyond their lifetimes. The best safeguard is to know the Bible well, to be able to reason and compare people's claims against scriptural standards. Prayerful discernment is a key. Remember that all teachings have some element of truth, but we must remember Jesus' words: "Watch out!" (v. 15).

REFLECTION QUESTIONS

1. Can you think of any false prophets who are around today? What makes you think that they are false teachers?

2. How can you best determine whether a teaching is true or false?

3. If someone you know shares with you a teaching that is inconsistent with Scripture, what is the best way to handle it?

29

EMPTY CONFESSION

MATTHEW 7:21–23

Jean Eugène Robert-Houdin is regarded as the first of the great showman magicians. His skills were so great that when France was having problems with the beginning of an uprising in their colony of Algeria, they called on him to help. In Algeria, a group of Muslim magicians called Marabouts were stirring up trouble. It was decided that Robert-Houdin could not only unmask the tricks of magicians, but also show that the French had more powerful magic.

One trick was particularly convincing. Calling a large, muscular man to the stage, he asked him if he could lift a small box that was sitting in front of him. The man easily lifted it over his head. After putting it down, Robert-Houdin challenged him, "I will make you as weak as one of your wives," then told him to lift it again. The man reached down as before, but was surprised to find that he couldn't move it. He grabbed it with two hands and pulled with all his might. Nothing. He continued but the box would not budge. Still determined, he tried again, but this time not only could he not move it, he also cried out and writhed in pain.

What the man did not know was that the night before, Robert-Houdin had rigged the small metal box with a strong electromagnet beneath it. After the magnet was turned on, the box was immovable.

The final time when the man grabbed the box, Robert-Houdin flipped a switch to allow electric current to flow, giving the man his first electric shock.[1] Robert-Houdin had fooled the people into thinking that the power was in his hands when it was something entirely different.

After Jesus talked about false prophets, He moved on to talking about counterfeit believers among the orthodox. Unlike false prophets, they believe and proclaim all the right doctrine and beliefs. They do not question the Bible or seek to put some new twist on Christ's teachings. In fact, they often accomplish a great deal of good.

Correct belief is important. Having an education and studying the original languages of the Bible is praiseworthy, and we are glad for those who give themselves to the discipline of study. The danger is that a person can learn historical contexts, the nuances of language, the fine points of doctrine, and still miss connection with the Lord.

Consider this scene from *Star Trek: The Next Generation*. Data, an android who desperately wanted to be human, played violin. When talking with Captain Picard about his flawless performance, Data shared that although his playing was technically proficient, he had been told by his fellow performers that he lacked soul.[2] The problem is the same when someone believes all the right things, but they have not put their heart into it or allowed the Lord to enter in.

People can involve themselves in all aspects of ministry from music to pastoral to preaching. Laypersons can teach a Sunday school class, serve as deacons, and faithfully give their tithe. Ministers can visit their flocks, work with their church staff, preach well-researched sermons, and preside over growing congregations. These are very good things. But people can also fall into the trap of doing them in a rote, mechanical way. Or simply doing them because others expect it, not because they care. Service that is rendered from an unsurrendered heart is only what it appears to be in the moment of execution.

Sometimes an entire congregation may commit the sin of living out their faith with their heads rather than their hearts. A church can have a range of helpful programs, community outreach, flawless music, and warm fellowship. The services can be scripted as seamless performances that leave the audience breathless. There can even be a feeling of joy and such anticipation that people hate to miss a week.

But are lives changed? Is there growth in the believers? If that church were swallowed by the earth, would there be any sense of loss from its vanished spiritual impact? Would people scratch their heads as they went by and wonder what used to be there?

Not one preacher, pastor, or layperson is free from the danger of a performance mentality. Not one denomination is beyond the risk of having congregations of this sort. There is no church that can't devolve to the level of being more like a little community theater than a living part of Christ's body.

Dietrich Bonhoeffer challenged his readers, "Here we are at last, here is the secret we have been waiting for since the Sermon on the Mount began. Here is the crucial question—has Jesus known us or not?"[3]

The sad thing is that too many will not realize how far off the mark they have been until the day of judgment when they face the Lord. They will cry out, "Lord, Lord, did we not prophesy in your name and in your name drive out demons and in your name perform many miracles?" (v. 22). The anguish of that moment is almost too much to imagine. Did we not . . . did we not . . . did we not . . . ?

The Lord's pronouncement to them shouts finality. "I never knew you. Away from me, you evildoers!" (v. 23). We must realize we cannot do the work of Christ without the Spirit of Christ. We can work for the Lord day and night and still not be His. In the end, what matters is that we are His more than the programs and evaluations we present. Counterfeit money looks real, feels real, and can fool many people. But in the end, it is worthless. So are counterfeit Christians.

REFLECTION QUESTIONS

1. How can someone avoid being a counterfeit Christian?

2. Which Christian practices or disciplines are easy to "perform" without the heart being in it? Why do you think that is?

3. How can we know whether a professing Christian is really living for the Lord?

30

SANDY OR SOLID

MATTHEW 7:24–29

When I was still a young Salvation Army officer, I was sent out as part of a group to respond to a hurricane near Panama City, Florida. The hurricane was fairly minimal, but it still did some substantial damage. The worst of it was in the town of Panama City Beach. One particular scene remains fresh in my memory. Apparently, one of the hotels was built too close to the water. The guests loved it because it was right on the beach, but when the storm waves came, the sand underneath the hotel eroded. The building split right down the middle, collapsing in on itself. Foolishly, the foundation was on the sand.

As Jesus concluded the Sermon on the Mount, He gave His listeners an illustration of what it means to be a true believer compared to being a believer for show. He focused on this critical issue several times throughout the sermon. He spoke about hypocrites who present faces to the world that are quite different from their real faces. Often, hypocrites aren't trying to deceive people as much as attempting to keep their feet in both worlds. Their hearts are divided, shifting from one place to another according to circumstance or what best fits the moment. Jesus wanted His listeners to understand that the Christian life is not a stage production. It is a battle of life and death, a path that is narrow and can be missed if we are not paying attention.

When we consider Christ's illustration about the two builders and the homes they constructed, it's interesting that their houses would have looked nearly identical to the casual passerby. They looked good, and the residents probably seemed happy with them. On a sunshiny day with gentle breezes blowing, you'd find no cause for alarm.

The difference was in the way they were built. The house on the sand was more easily constructed, with less trouble and less cost. Perhaps it was easier to access or commanded a better view. Move a little sand, smooth it over, and outline the walls on top of it. Done.

Building on the rock was more difficult. The house wasn't just perched there; foundation work had to be done. The builders probably found it arduous to chip away at the stone in order to dig into it. It would have been a slow, frustrating task. In fact, the foundation may have been the most difficult part of the house to construct, and when it was finished, it was invisible to the naked eye.

Herein is the difference in how we build our lives on the Lord. If we are not going to be bothered with a firm foundation, then anywhere we choose to land is fine. Go for the scenic view, the easy access.

But if we are to have a foundation, if we are to build wisely, we should realize that much of the work will happen in a secret place, hidden away from the eyes of others. Here is where prayer battles are won. Here is where dwelling in the Word occurs. Here is where we chip away to know about the Lord we adore, to seek Him in quiet moments, to listen as He speaks, not with a billboard, but with a gentle whisper. No one will know how much we labored to build our foundation. And when we make our appearance to the world outside, it won't be noticed. On sunny days, this house will stand no better than the one constructed on sand.

But that is not where the value of the construction is proved. Jesus told of a violent storm that came to assault the homes of both the foolish and the wise. These storms of life are often unexpected in their timing and their level of ferocity. Even in the home of the wise, the cyclone can hit with such force as to make one wonder whether anything will be left by morning.

What form do these storms take? Everyone loses someone near and dear to them. We are not allowed the luxury of deciding what time is best to have someone taken from our side. Death comes when it comes, convenient or not, giving us time to prepare or not. Illness comes. We might pop vitamins and jog hours a day, but we have no guarantee that our bodies will not betray us. Pain visits in the form and strength it chooses.

Relationships can fail. The risk of love is that the more we love, the more potential there is for our beloved to hurt us. Vulnerability is the price of merging our life with that of another; this is true with spouses, with children, and with anyone else. Although it isn't always intentional, relationships wax and wane.

We experience attacks on our faith. We wonder when we hear of someone's prayer being miraculously answered while ours seems to merit only God's silence. Doubts nag and nip at us like some tiny dog. We can become profoundly confused about matters of faith during the course of our lives when we know we have given ourselves fully to God, yet still find ourselves confused and feeling a little lost.

The storms come. They sweep in, and while some pass quickly, others lengthen their assaults, testing the mettle of the building. The fool builds on sand, and when the sand erodes, the life falls apart in ruin. But the person who has met the Lord in secret, who has constructed a foundation on Him, the Rock of Ages, finds that He will sustain them.

At the end of the storm we might find ourselves a little worse for wear, but it will be clear that we are bowed but not broken, attacked but not defeated.

REFLECTION QUESTIONS

1. In what ways do people build their lives foolishly?

2. How have you built your foundation? How will it stand in the storms of life?

3. How does the Sermon on the Mount relate to building a strong foundation?

NOTES

INTRODUCTION

1. Oswald Chambers, *Studies in the Sermon on the Mount* (Grand Rapids: Discovery House Publishers, 1995), 13.

DEVOTION 1

1. E. Stanley Jones, *The Christ of the Mount: A Working Philosophy of Life* (Whitefish, MT: Kessinger Publishing, 1931), 57.

DEVOTION 3

1. Clifton Fadiman and André Bernard, eds., *Bartlett's Book of Anecdotes* (Boston, MA: Little, Brown & Company, 1985), 98.

2. D. Martyn Lloyd-Jones, *Studies in the Sermon on the Mount, vol. 1* (Grand Rapids, MI: Wm. B. Eerdmans Publishing Co., 1971), 68.

DEVOTION 4

1. James Montgomery Boice, *The Sermon on the Mount* (Grand Rapids, MI: Baker Book House, 2006), 40.

2. Sinclair B. Ferguson, *The Sermon on the Mount* (Carlisle, PA: Banner of Truth Trust, 1987), 27.

3. John Wesley and Kenneth Cain Kinghorn, ed., *John Wesley on the Sermon on the Mount* (Nashville, TN: Abingdon Press, 2002), 66.

DEVOTION 5

1. Michael P. Green, ed., *1500 Illustrations for Biblical Preaching* (Grand Rapids, MI: Baker Book House, 2000), 240.

2. Leonard Roy Frank, ed., *Quotationary* (New York City, NY: Random House, 2001), 506.

3. Harold Begbie, *The Life of General William Booth, vol. 2* (West Nyack, NY: The Salvation Army Eastern Territory, 2005), 77.

DEVOTION 6

1. Craig Brian Larson and Phyllis Ten Elshof, eds., *1001 Illustrations that Connect* (Grand Rapids, MI: Zondervan, 2008), 80–81.

2. D. Martyn Lloyd-Jones, *Studies in the Sermon on the Mount, vol. 1* (Grand Rapids, MI: Wm. B. Eerdmans Publishing Co., 1971), 115.

3. Allen Satterlee, ed., *Notable Quotables* (Atlanta, GA: The Salvation Army, 1985), 166.

DEVOTION 7

1. D. Martyn Lloyd-Jones, *Studies in the Sermon on the Mount, vol. 1* (Grand Rapids, MI: Wm. B. Eerdmans Publishing Co., 1971), 122.

2. D. A. Carson, *Jesus' Sermon on the Mount and His Confrontation with the World* (Grand Rapids, MI: Baker Book House, 2004), 28.

DEVOTION 8

1. Stoyan Zaimov, "21 Coptic Christians Beheaded by ISIS Honored for Refusing to Deny Christ," *The Christian Post, Washington, DC,* February 16, 2017, https://www.christianpost.com/news/21-coptic-christians-beheaded-by-isis-honored-refusing-deny-christ-175128.

2. Cristina Maza, "Christian Persecution and Genocide is Worse Now Than 'Any Time in History,' Report Says," *Newsweek, New*

York, NY, January 4, 2018, http://www.newsweek.com/christian-persecution-genocide-worse-ever-770462.

3. F. B. Meyer, *Blessed are Ye: Talks on the Beatitudes* (Greenville, SC: Emerald House Group Incorporated, 1998), 122.

4. James Montgomery Boice, *The Sermon on the Mount* (Grand Rapids, MI: Baker Book House, 2006), 53.

5. George B. Smith, *The Christian Charter* (London: Salvationist Supplies and Purchasing, 1972), 25.

6. E. Stanley Jones, *The Christ of the Mount: A Working Philosophy of Life* (Whitefish, MT: Kessinger Publishing, 1931), 82.

7. John Wesley and Kenneth Cain Kinghorn, ed., *John Wesley on the Sermon on the Mount* (Nashville, TN: Abingdon Press, 2002), 98.

DEVOTION 9

1. John R. W. Stott, *The Message of the Sermon on the Mount* (Downers Grove, IL: InterVarsity Press, 1978), 60.

DEVOTION 10

1. Craig Brian Larson and Phyllis Ten Elshof, eds., *1001 Illustrations that Connect* (Grand Rapids, MI: Zondervan, 2008), 75.

2. John R. W. Stott, *The Message of the Sermon on the Mount* (Downers Grove, IL: Intervarsity Press, 1978), 63.

3. Por Yong Ming, "What Percentage of the Light Spectrum are Humans Able to See With Their Eyes?," *Quora*, April 19, 2017, https://www.quora.com/What-percentage-of-the-light-spectrum-are-humans-able-to-see-with-their-eyes.

4. John Wesley and Kenneth Cain Kinghorn, editor, *John Wesley on the Sermon on the Mount* (Nashville, TN: Abingdon Press, 2002), 114.

DEVOTION 11

1. Tony Evans, *Tony Evans' Book of Illustrations* (Chicago, IL: Moody Publishers, 2009), 183.

2. Dietrich Bonhoeffer, *The Cost of Discipleship* (New York City, New York: Macmillan Company Publishing Co., Inc., 1961), 137-138.

3. Sinclair B. Ferguson, *The Sermon on the Mount* (Carlisle, PA: Banner of Truth Trust, 1987), 72–73.

4. John Wesley and Kenneth Cain Kinghorn, editor, *John Wesley on the Sermon on the Mount* (Nashville, TN: Abingdon Press, 2002), 132.

DEVOTION 12

1. Jeffrey Kluger, "America's Anger Is Out of Control," *Time*, June 1, 2016, http://time.com/4353606/anger-america-enough-already.

2. Cited by John R. W. Stott, *The Message of the Sermon on the Mount* (Downers Grove, IL: Intervarsity Press, 1978), 84.

3. Carl G. Vaught, *The Sermon on the Mount: A Theological Investigation* (Waco, TX: Baylor University Press, 2001), 65.

DEVOTION 13

1. Tony Evans, *Tony Evans' Book of Illustrations* (Chicago, IL: Moody Publishers, 2009), 278.

2. Carl G. Vaught, *The Sermon on the Mount: A Theological Investigation* (Waco, TX: Baylor University Press, 2001), 74.

3. John R. W. Stott, *The Message of the Sermon on the Mount* (Downers Grove, IL: Intervarsity Press, 1978), 88.

4. Jonathan T. Pennington, *The Sermon on the Mount and Human Flourishing: A Theological Commentary* (Grand Rapids, MI: Baker Academic Books, 2017), 191.

DEVOTION 14

1. Bob Sullivan, "Identity Theft Hit an All-Time High in 2016," *USA Today*, Feb 6, 2017, https://www.usatoday.com/story/money/personalfinance/2017/02/06/identity-theft-hit-all-time-high-2016/97398548.

2. E. Stanley Jones, *The Christ of the Mount: A Working Philosophy of Life* (Whitefish, MT: Kessinger Publishing, 1931), 163.

3. Dietrich Bonhoeffer, *The Cost of Discipleship* (New York City, New York: Macmillan Company Publishing Co., Inc., 1961), 153.

DEVOTION 15

1. Sinclair B. Ferguson, *The Sermon on the Mount* (Carlisle, PA: Banner of Truth Trust, 1987), 99.

2. Ferguson, *The Sermon on the Mount*, 100.

3. E. Stanley Jones, *The Christ of the Mount: A Working Philosophy of Life* (Whitefish, MT: Kessinger Publishing, 1931), 171.

4. Dr. O.S. Hawkins, "Go the Second Mile," *Faith Gateway,* April 28, 2016, http://www.faithgateway.com/go-the-second-mile-matthew-5-41/#.WntgdIJG2Rs.

5. Jamie Buckingham, *The Last Word*, Kindle version (Palm Bay, FL: Risky Living Ministries, Inc.), 2016, Location 997-1024.

DEVOTION 16

1. Pat Leonard, "The Angel of Marye's Heights," *The New York Times,* December 14, 2012, https://opinionator.blogs.nytimes.com/2012/12/14/the-angel-of-maryes-heights.

2. Carl G. Vaught, *The Sermon on the Mount: A Theological Investigation* (Waco, TX: Baylor University Press, 2001), 107.

3. Dietrich Bonhoeffer, *The Cost of Discipleship* (New York City, New York: Macmillan Company Publishing Co., Inc., 1961), 165.

4. *Wikepedia,* https://en.wikipedia.org/wiki/West_Nickel_Mines_School_shooting.

DEVOTION 18

1. Clifton Fadiman and André Bernard, eds., *Bartlett's Book of Anecdotes* (Boston, MA: Little, Brown & Company, 1985), 567.

2. D. A. Carson, *Jesus' Sermon on the Mount and His Confrontation with the World* (Grand Rapids, MI: Baker Book House, 2004), 60.

3. Carl G. Vaught, *The Sermon on the Mount: A Theological Investigation* (Waco, TX: Baylor University Press, 2001), 119.

4. John R. W. Stott, *The Message of the Sermon on the Mount* (Downers Grove, IL: Intervarsity Press, 1978), 129.

5. Stott, *The Message of the Sermon on the Mount*, 129–130.

DEVOTION 19

1. Tony Evans, *Tony Evans' Book of Illustrations* (Chicago, IL: Moody Publishers, 2009), 231.

2. James Montgomery, *The Song Book of The Salvation Army* (Alexandria, VA: The Salvation Army National Headquarters, 2016), 230-231.

3. James Montgomery Boice, *The Sermon on the Mount* (Grand Rapids, MI: Baker Book House, 2006), 169.

DEVOTION 20

1. Clifton Fadiman and André Bernard, eds., *Bartlett's Book of Anecdotes* (Boston, MA: Little, Brown & Company, 1985), 346.

2. D. A. Carson, *Jesus' Sermon on the Mount and His Confrontation with the World* (Grand Rapids, MI: Baker Book House, 2004), 72.

3. Allen Satterlee, ed., *Notable Quotables* (Atlanta, GA: The Salvation Army, 1985), 157.

DEVOTION 21

1. Craig Brian Larson, *Leadership Journal, 750 Engaging Illustrations* (Grand Rapids, MI: Baker Book House, 2007), 181.

2. "Anger-how it affects people," https://www.betterhealth.vic.gov.au/health/healthyliving/anger-how-it-affects-people, Accessed May 1, 2018.

DEVOTION 22

1. Allen Satterlee, ed., *Notable Quotables* (Atlanta, GA: The Salvation Army, 1985), 191.

2. J. D. Douglas and Merrill C. Tenney, Moisés Silva, ed., *Zondervan Illustrated Bible Dictionary* (Grand Rapids, MI: Zondervan, 2011), 471.

3. Carl G. Vaught, *The Sermon on the Mount: A Theological Investigation* (Waco, TX: Baylor University Press, 2001), 136–137.

DEVOTION 23

1. Craig Brian Larson and *Leadership Journal*, *750 Engaging Illustrations* (Grand Rapids, MI: Baker Book House, 2007), 356.

2. D. A. Carson, *Jesus' Sermon on the Mount and His Confrontation with the World* (Grand Rapids, MI: Baker Book House, 2004), 84.

3. Carl G. Vaught, *The Sermon on the Mount: A Theological Investigation* (Waco, TX: Baylor University Press, 2001), 144.

4. James Montgomery Boice, *The Sermon on the Mount* (Grand Rapids, MI: Baker Book House, 2006), 216.

5. Francis Bacon, *Goodreads,* https://www.goodreads.com/quotes/446478-money-is-a-great-servant-but-a-bad-master. Accessed February 9, 2018.

DEVOTION 24

1. Michael P. Green, ed., *1500 Illustrations for Biblical Preaching* (Grand Rapids, MI: Baker Book House, 2000), 407.

DEVOTION 25

1. E. Stanley Jones, *The Christ of the Mount: A Working Philosophy of Life* (Whitefish, MT: Kessinger Publishing, 1931), 245.

2. James Montgomery Boice, *The Sermon on the Mount* (Grand Rapids, MI: Baker Book House, 2006), 225.

3. J. D. Douglas and Merrill C. Tenney, Moisés Silva, ed., *Zondervan Illustrated Bible Dictionary* (Grand Rapids, MI: Zondervan, 2011), 74.

4. D. A. Carson, *Jesus' Sermon on the Mount and His Confrontation with the World* (Grand Rapids, MI: Baker Book House, 2004), 112.

DEVOTION 26

1. Michael P. Green, ed., *1500 Illustrations for Biblical Preaching* (Grand Rapids, MI: Baker Book House, 2000), 275.

2. Carl G. Vaught, *The Sermon on the Mount: A Theological Investigation* (Waco, TX: Baylor University Press, 2001), 170.

3. Leonard Roy Frank, ed., *Quotationary* (New York City, NY: Random House, 2001), 636.

4. John R. W. Stott, *The Message of the Sermon on the Mount* (Downers Grove, IL: Intervarsity Press, 1978), 186.

DEVOTION 27

1. "What Americans Believe about Universalism and Pluralism," *Barna Group,* April 18, 2011, https://www.barna.com/research/what-americans-believe-about-universalism-and-pluralism/.

2. Ira Stanphill, "Follow Me," (Singspiration Music, 1953).

DEVOTION 28

1. "Jim Jones" https://en.wikipedia.org/wiki/Jim_Jones. Accessed February 10, 2018.

2. John R. W. Stott, *The Message of the Sermon on the Mount* (Downers Grove, IL: Intervarsity Press, 1978), 200.

DEVOTION 29

1. "The French Magician Who Squelched a Revolt," *rense.com*, April 11, 2008, http://www.rense.com/general81/rfr.htm.

2. "The Ensigns of Command." *Star Trek: The Next Generation*. Paramount Studios. Released October 2, 1989. Television.

3. Dietrich Bonhoeffer, *The Cost of Discipleship* (New York City, New York: Macmillan Company Publishing Co., Inc., 1961), 217.